fíe
shore

This book deals with day-to-day life on the Aran islands at the turn of the century, a lifestyle that is a significant part of the Irish heritage. It is a social history and an anthropology.

It deals first with farming and fishing: the human organisation of the land — field patterns, stone walls, crops and animals; work on the sea — the currach and the Galway hooker; the harvesting of fertilizer, kelp and wrack from the seashore. It includes the beliefs, customs and superstitions associated with farming and fishing.

Then it describes building a house and making a home. There is a section on clothes – the sweaters and stockings, the crios, the pampooties – and how they were made.

Social events demanded special activities and these are described — singing, house walking, weddings, death.

Family structure, family relationships and kinship patterns are outlined, and particular attention is paid to the experience of emigration, a common feature of island life.

There is a section on modern Aran life contrasting it with the traditional patterns.

O'BRIEN ISLAND BOOKS INCLUDE:
Aran Series: A World of Stone, Field and Shore, Island Stories.
The Blasket Islands and Blasket Island Guide (Stagles).
Skellig (Lavelle), Saltees (Roche & Merne),
Inishmurray (Heraughty).

Frist published 1977 by O'Brien Educational Ltd., 20 Victoria Road, Dublin 6
Reprinted 1980, 1982, 1985, 1987, 1989, 1993.

10 9 8 7 6

Printed by The Guernsey Press Co. Ltd.

ISBN 0 905140 13 3

The Curriculum Development Unit was established in 1972. It is funded by the City of Dublin Vocational Education Committee. It is managed jointly by the City of Dublin Vocational Education Committee, Trinity College, Dublin, and the Department of Education. This book forms part of the Humanities Curriculum.

Unit Director:	Anton Trant	
Deputy Director:	Tony Crooks	
Humanities Team:		
Tony Crooks	Coordinator 1972-79	
Nora Godwin	1973-79	
	Coordinator 1979-	
Agnes McMahon	1975-76	
Bernard O'Flaherty	1976-78	
Dermot Stokes	1977-82	
Ann Treacy	1978-80	
Patricia McCarthy	1984-	

This collection has been researched and edited by Paul O'Sullivan with revisions by Nora Godwin.

Prior to publication, the following schools were involved in the development, use and revision of the collection. The suggestions and comments of the teachers in these schools have been used as a basis for the edition.
Colaiste Dhulaigh, Coolock; Colaiste Eanna, Cabra; Colaiste Eoin, Finglas; Coolmine Community School, Clonsilla; Gonzaga College, Dublin; Liberties Vocational School, Dublin; Scoil Ide, Finglas; Vocational School, Ballyfermot; Vocational School for Boys, Clogher Road; Vocational School, Crumlin Road.

contents

*Readers Note
The text from pages 84 to 146
of Field and Shore, although
written in the present tense, is
set around 1900.*

the land
of aran

THE ARAN ISLANDS AND the Burren district of North Clare are perhaps the most barren parts of Ireland. Cromwell is reputed to have said that one could not "find a tree to hang a man, water to drown him nor earth to bury him" in these areas. Yet, one who had a bird's eye view of the Aran Islands could clearly see the outline of ancient fields especially around the great stone forts which are scattered over the islands.

We can only guess that, at some time in the distant past, the land was much better than it has been in recent centuries. The islands may even have been covered by forests or leafy deciduous trees. It seems likely that the clearing of the trees allowed heavy rainfall and strong winds to wash the soil off the rocky limestone surface. Man may have helped to destroy the fertility of the soil by over-use and bad management. Whatever the reason, the surface of the Aran islands, now, is a series of bare limestone terraces. To grow their crops the islanders must make their fields on the bare rocks.

An Aran poet, Tomás Ó Díreáin, describes the struggle of the island farmer to make his barren land fertile.

The Aran Landscape. Bare limestone pavements, criss-crossed by fissures step up gently to a hilltop fort.

AN tÁRANNACH

Féach é ina sheasamh ar an leic,　　*Le allas a bhaithis,*
A tá liath agus lom,　　*Le fuil a chroí,*
Ag guí chun Dia　　*Déanfaidh sé talamh*
Le neart agus stuaim　　*As na scalpachaí.*
Go gcuirfidh sé toradh
(Le anró agus pian)　　*Tomás Ó Direáin*
Ar an áit atá lom
Leis na mílte bliain.

These maps show how one townland near Kilronan has had more and more of its open rough pasture improved to make new fields.

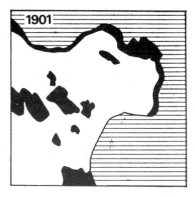

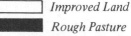
Improved Land
Rough Pasture

MAKING FIELDS

An area of flat rock which is in a suitable location is chosen The surface is evened by knocking off any outcrops of rock, but i must not be completely smooth or the soil which is to be spread on it will not be able to grip and will be blown away.

Large cracks are filled up with pieces of rock to prevent the soi from trickling down through them. The larger stones, which wer removed from the surface are used to build a wall around th 'field'. This wall will give shelter to the crops growing in th field as well as keeping out any wandering cattle or sheep.

The surface which has been prepared is then covered with layer of sand and seaweed carted up from the beach. Finally a layer o precious soil is laid on top. This soil has been gathered from th crevices between the rocks and from the more fertile parts of th island.

The writer J. M. Synge visited the Aran Islands each summe from 1898 – 1902. Here he writes about the making of a field

"The other day the men of this house made a new field. There was a slight bank of earth under the wall of the yard and another in the corner of the cabbage garden. The old man and his eldest son dug out the clay, with the care of men working in a gold-mine and Michael packed it in panniers – there are no wheeled vehicle on this island – for transport to a flat rock in a sheltered corner o the holding, where it was mixed with sand and seaweed and spread out in a layer upon the stone. Most of the potato growing of the island is carried on in fields of this sort – for which the people pay a considerable rent – and if the season is at all dry, their hope of a fair crop is nearly always disappointed.

It is now nine days since rain has fallen, and the people are filled with anxiety, although the sun has not yet been hot enough to do harm."

In some parts of the islands the area used for growing crops is gradually increasing as new fields are added each year. A field may be sown with potatoes as its first crop, then spend a year under a crop of rye and finally be allowed to lie fallow, or rest, for a year or two. This system is called a crop rotation – each crop follows the previous one in a set order and it is a valuable means of preserving the fertility of the soil.

Tiny stone walled fields on Inisheer. There are no gateways and a farmer will knock down and rebuild sections of a wall to allow his cows to enter and leave a pasture.

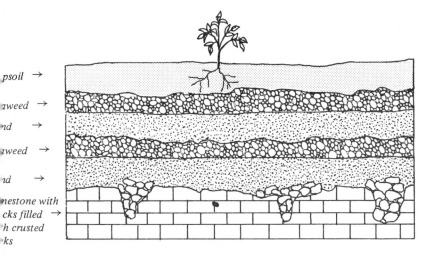

topsoil →

seaweed →

sand →

seaweed →

sand →

limestone with cracks filled with crusted rocks →

LAND OWNERSHIP

Each family on Aran owns its farm. This was not always so as the islanders were, until this century, tenant farmers who had to pay rent to a landlord for their small holdings. In the 1870's a series of poor harvests, especially of potatoes and oats, meant that the tenants were short of food and were unable to pay their rent to the landlords. Evictions took place in Mayo and Galway and other parts of the country and the tenants were compelled to unite to fight for their rights. In 1879 they formed the Land League to campaign for "The Three F's" —

> "Fair Rent
> Fixity of Tenure
> Freedom of Sale"

They were granted these demands by the British Parliament in Gladstone's Land Acts of 1881 and 1882. Under these acts a tenant and his family could remain on their farm even if the rent was in arrears and they also had the right to sell their interest in the farm to any other person. But the members of the Land League had tasted victory and had acquired a new aim. They now wished to get rid of landlords altogether and make each man the sole owner of his farm. The Government of the United Kingdom was forced to accept this proposal and made money available at low interest rates to the tenants so that they could buy out their holdings. The landlords were only too happy to agree and to cut their losses. By 1910, four million hectares of Irish land had changed hands under these purchase schemes. But the process of reform was slow in some areas. It was not until 1922 that the landlords, the Digby-St. Lawrence family, sold their interests in the islands and the Aran farmers became the owners of their land. Each pays a small annuity as repayment on the Land Act loan he received.

FARM AND FAMILY

The father in each family is the one who makes all the important decisions regarding the farm. His sons work beside him and learn the skills of farming from him. When he grows old he hands over the farm to one of his sons, usually the eldest, when the young man is ready for marriage. The father and mother allow the young couple to take over the running of both the farm and the house and they 'retire' from control. This arrangement often works out very well and all concerned are happy. Sometimes, though, an old man may be slow to give up control of his farm and may hang on to it until both he and his sons are quite old.

The sons often feel bitter in such a situation because, without the farm they do not have the independence and security to get married. Island men usually do not marry until they are quite old; in many cases the man is forty years of age before he has the independence to enable him to marry. Sadly, some men wait too long for a parent to hand over the land or to die, and find that they are too old to marry when they eventually receive their inheritance. Not all young people are prepared to wait; some prefer to emigrate and give up their claim to the farm completely.

Parents are not always at fault, of course. The young couple may become too bossy or may not pay enough regard to the knowledge, experience and age of the old couple. Friction between the old mother and the young wife is regarded by the islanders as a great misfortune. They know that it can make for a very unhappy household.

In Aran, land is fairly evenly divided among the farmers, each holding consisting of 7 to 8 hectares. Most farmers also own a portion of sea-shore where they can gather seaweed for fertilizer. Each person has some good fields suitable for growing his potatoes and grazing his cattle. In addition he has some rough grazing for sheep and some of the almost useless bare stone flagging. This means, of course, that a man's fields may be widely scattered. Such a farm is described as fragmented.

FIELD PATTERNS

Distinctive field patterns are found in different parts of Ireland and they are an important clue to the type of farming carried on locally. In the fertile grazing lands of Meath, farms are large and the density of population is low. Fields are also large in order to facilitate the grazing of cattle. But in West Galway and the Aran Islands the land is poor and the farms are very small. The irregular pattern of tiny stone walled fields reflects this.

STONE WALLS

Each little field is surrounded by a stone wall. The walls are quite high, forming a maze for the stranger who can find himself going round in circles. The walls are a convenient place where the

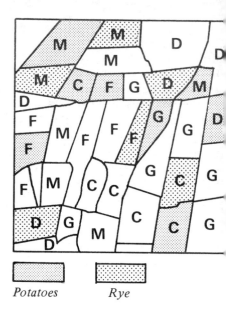

Potatoes   Rye

This diagram shows a 28 hectare section of one of the islands. There are forty fields in all owned by five different farmers. The owner of each field is identified by the initial letter of his name on the map.

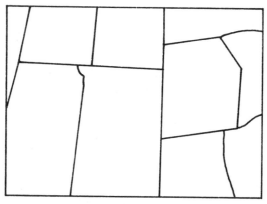

Left shows a field pattern in Co. Meath, where the fields are large compared to the small fields of Aran

½ KM

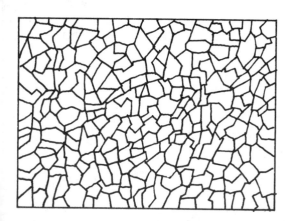

farmer can put the rocks and boulders which he clears from his land. They also protect the precious soil and crops in each field from the strong Atlantic winds. The walls are modern examples of the dry stone masonry found in the ancient forts. No mortar or cement is used in their building. The stones are carefully selected and positioned so that the wind may pass freely through the gaps between them. In this way the wall can withstand the fierce force of the south westerly gales. Wind passing through the walls often makes an eerie whistling sound over the islands.

GATES

Metal and timber must be imported from the mainland and so are in short supply on the islands. Therefore 'gates' in the walls are also made of rocks. When a wall is being built, an entrance gap, several feet wide, is left open. When the wall is completed the gap is filled with rounded stones. Each time a farmer wishes to drive his cattle into the field he knocks down this 'gate'. The rounded stones tumble down quite easily and can be rebuilt without much trouble, afterwards.

CROPS

The little fields produce potatoes and rye, mainly for use on the islands. Vegetables such as cabbage, onions and lettuce are sometimes grown in little plots of land around the houses. Here and there, willows, for basket making, are grown in small enclosures.

Potatoes are the most common crop in Aran, and as in the rest of the country, they are a staple in the diet of the people. The potato is easily grown and thrives in a damp climate. It has an extremely high yield and even poor land will produce up to 15 tonnes per hectare. This makes it an attractive crop for the small farmer who has a limited amount of land available for tillage. In addition, the potato has a very high food value and, combined with milk, bread, fish and meat, makes for a nourishing, well-balanced diet. In large, fertile fields potatoes are sown with the aid of a horse-drawn plough in long, single rows. But in the small, stony fields of Aran the potatoes must be sown by manual labour. Using only a spade the farmer plants his potatoes in wide ridges known as lazybeds. First of all, narrow trenches, about 50 centimetres in width, are dug with a spade. The trenches are spaced over 1 metre intervals and layers of seaweed are spread on the ground between each pair. Sods from the trench are turned over, grassy side down, on top of the seaweed, to build up a 'ridge'. The rotting of the grass and seaweed will provide vital nutrients to feed the growing crop. More seaweed and, finally, a layer of soil are added. The potato seeds are planted in this top layer, in rows of three or four.

Two months after planting, more soil is dug from the trenches and added to the ridge to protect and strengthen the young plants. The potato patch may be weeded several times and when the potato stalks have attained their full height they will be sprayed with a mixture of bluestone and water to prevent blight.

The potato seed is selected in mid January. Potatoes retained from the previous crop are cut into sections, each of which must have an 'eye'. The fields are prepared and planting or 'seeding' takes place in March and early April. It is very important for the islanders to sow potatoes on time. "A person who is lazy about planting, is lazy about everything" they say. A farmer who is late with his 'seeding' is contemptuously referred to as a "Cuckoo farmer" because he is still seeding when the first call of the cuckoo is heard in May.

Potatoes are harvested from the end of July onwards. They are sorted in the fields into seed potatoes, cattle feed, and high quality potatoes for human consumption. They are stored in outhouses or in pits until needed. A pit is a shallow trench in which the potatoes are placed. They are covered over with hay or straw and finally with a layer of earth or sods. The potatoes will then be safe from both frost and field animals. Only in a very wet year does the crop yield a surplus beyond the family's immediate needs. This surplus, when it occurs, is sold on the mainland.

Rye is the only grain crop grown on the islands. It thrives in a damp, cool climate and grows well even on soils which are poor and thin. The tough rye straw is used for thatching the island houses and is also used as a bedding and a feeding stuff for cattle. The grain yield is sufficient only to provide seed for next year's planting.

The rye crop is sown in autumn, after the potatoes have been lifted. Most farmers rotate their potato and rye crops in order to allow the soil to renew the different nutrients which each crop drains from it. Harvesting takes place in June.

Rye, which is to be used for thatching, is pulled rather than cut. It is tied in bundles and propped against a wall to dry in the

Above — The method of making lazybeds for growing potatoes. The soil is cut and turned back on itself.
Below — Lazybeds in a potato garden in Inisheer in early Summer. In the background is the 15th century O'Brien Castle and the outline of Dun Formna which surrounds it.

summer sun. The islanders prefer to pull the rye because the roots, which remain attached to the straw, prevent the bundles from slipping when they are laid on a roof for use by the thatcher.

The dry bundles of rye are threshed to separate the grain from the stalks. Two large stones are stood on end, leaning against each other. The bundles, or sheaves, are beaten individually, against the stones until the grain falls away. This is known as *flailing.* The seed is still wrapped in a dry skin called chaff. It is dropped, a handful at a time onto a dry, flat rock surface, while the wind blows the chaff away. This is known as *winnowing.* The grain is used as seed for the next year's crop.

If the rye is to be used as an animal feed it is cut, using a scythe, while it is still 'green' and has not, as yet, ripened fully. The farmer rakes it into parallel rows for drying, turning it every now and then. When dry, it is carefully stacked in ricks which are tied down with strong grass ropes, *súgáns,* to prevent them blowing away.

The harvesting of the crops is the most vital activity in the yearly cycle of farmwork. It is a time of worry and anxiety for the farmer because bad weather can delay the harvest or prevent the rye from drying properly, making it useless for its intended purpose.

When all the crops have been harvested, great celebrations take place. The spade is ceremoniously placed in the fire for a few moments, to show that it is no longer needed. The helpers and neighbours who have assisted in the harvest are invited to a *féil searra* — a céilí to mark the successful end to a year's work on the land.

FARM ANIMALS

The visitor to Aran is frequently impressed by the fact that each farmer keeps one or more cows, even though the farms are tiny, the land poor and grass extremely scarce. Cattle are very highly valued on the islands. The size of a farm is seldom described in acres. The islanders prefer to say "He has the grass of two cows."

Cattle are grazed on scattered patches of grassland which have been cordoned off for the purpose. They are left in the fields all year round, despite the bad weather. During a severe winter, when there is not enough grass to graze on, the farmer will carry bundles of rye to the fields for his cows. When nothing else is available, he may even feed them on a mixture of bran and

Above— Goats are kept by many families. They seek out patches of grass and are an important part of the economy, providing milk and hides.

Left — Cows are seldom housed in a byre on Aran, but are left in the fields both Summer and Winter. A common sight is that of women or young men coming or going from distant fields with a milk-can.

potatoes. Cattle must be very sturdy to survive in the harsh environment of the islands. The young calf is allowed to suckle its mother's milk for a much longer period than is common on the mainland. Though this means less milk for themselves, the islanders feel that it is worthwhile in order to rear a strong fat calf.

One or more dairy cows supply the milk requirements of each household. The cows are milked in the fields, which are often at a considerable distance from the farmhouse. Each milch cow yields little more than 1800 litres per annum due to the harsh conditions and poor grass. Whereas, in a fertile area like the Golden Vale a cow may yield twice this quantity. Some of this milk is fed to calves; some of it is churned at home to make butter; most of it is consumed in liquid form.

Cattle are sold at regular fairs held on all three islands. Sales are highest in the early summer and at the great Michaelmas fairs held on the 28th September. The farmers sell off their surplus stock at this time as grass will probably be scarce during the winter. The buyers, or cattle jobbers as they are called, come from Galway, and they take the animals to the mainland for fattening on good grassland before exporting them to England.

Horses are also sold at these fairs and pigs may be disposed of at regular intervals or slaughtered and salted down for home consumption.

Sheep and goats are also kept by many farmers on the islands. These animals are well suited to Aran. They are allowed to roam freely over the rough pastures and rocky hills seeking out grass in the crevices between the slabs of limestone. Sheep supply meat and, more importantly wool. The goats provide milk and hides. Some farmers also keep pigs which are housed in enclosures in the farmyard and are fed on boiled potatoes, domestic scraps and skimmed milk left over after buttermaking.

The donkey is the favourite beast of burden on the islands. He is sure footed and nimble on the rocky surface and he requires neither farm cart nor roadway. The farmer straps two wicker baskets, or panniers, across the donkey's back, and in these he transports seaweed from the shore and potatoes and rye from the fields. He may ride on the donkey when travelling to his outlying fields or hitch a small cart to the animal when collecting supplies from pier head or beach, after delivery by the steamer. Some horses and ponies are also kept but the versatile donkey is a more useful beast in such conditions.

Occasionally an islander may go to Galway to buy farm animals a cow, a donkey, or perhaps a horse. Getting an animal home) Inisheer or Inishmaan may pose a problem as the steamer innot come to land in either of these islands. The animals are :nerally hoisted by rope from the steamer's deck and gently •wered into the water behind a waiting curragh. Two men in the ern of the curragh hold the animal with a halter allowing it to wim ashore behind the boat. Smaller animals, such as pigs and 1eep, have their legs tied together and they are bundled into the urragh along with the rest of the cargo.

BELIEFS AND CUSTOMS

All over Ireland, particularly in areas where land is of poor uality, such as Aran, farmers practice age-old customs which are elieved to be of benefit in preserving the fertility of the land.

Bad luck is said to follow if a farmer misses out a line when lanting a ridge of potatoes. A fistful of salt may be sprinkled n a field to preserve the fertility of the soil.

If a funeral passes through a farm it brings bad luck to the ind but a goat, kept with a herd of cows, may bring good luck.

The first stream of milk from a newly calved cow is allowed to ill to the ground "for those who might need it".

Many customs and beliefs concerning the land are related ɔ particular times of the year. The feast of the Holy Innocents, á na Leanbh, falls on December 28th and is also known as The ross Day, Lá Crosta na Bliana. If, for instance, this feast happens ɔ occur on a Monday, then every Monday throughout that year ʻill be a 'Cross day'. It is regarded as unlucky to get married or to ig a grave on such a day and bad luck may follow if the planting r the harvesting of crops is begun on 'Cross day'.

Work which involves any actions of turning or twisting ncluding any form of digging, is never performed on St. Brigid's)ay — Bíonn Lá Le Bríde ina shaoire ar chasaibh, St. Brigid's Day ; free from twisting, the people say. A similar prohibition exists oncerning November 11th, St. Martin's Day.

On Good Friday, adults and weaned children never drink milk ut it is regarded as lucky to plant some seed potatoes on that ay. The Feast of St. John on 24th June corresponds to the ncient festival of Midsummer. On St. John's Eve bonfires are lit 1 every village and the farmers throw a blazing bush into the •otato gardens and rye fields to bring luck.

*Left – The 'steamer' taki
cow on board at Kilronan
transport to the mainland.*

*Below – The Cruel Sea – e:
ing a mighty force on
Atlantic coastlines of all t
islands. The bedding plane
limestones and shale can
identified in the sheer fac
the cliffs which rise in the b
ground.*

the sea

OR FIVE HUNDRED KILOMETRES the sea floor slopes gently westwards from the Irish coast before plunging abruptly to the ocean depths. This shallow submarine area is known as the Continental Shelf. The waters on the Continental Shelf are penetrated, almost to the very bottom, by the sun's rays. They are warmed by the current of the North Atlantic Drift, flowing across the ocean from the Gulf of Mexico. Hundreds of rivers and streams bring billions of tiny animals down to this sea. It is a rich feeding ground, teeming with many species of fish.

Most farmers on Aran are fishermen too. The sea has provided food for the islanders over the centuries. It has allowed them to supplement the meagre living which they wring from their rocky fields. It has protected them in times of invasion, and in hungry famine years it has given them the food which saved them from starvation. But the sea is also cruel. It has isolated the islanders, battering them with violent storms and cutting them off, over long periods, from human contact and medical aid. Time and again it has claimed the lives of the island men.

The islanders respect the sea, knowing the dangers of its ever changing moods. They know and understand the workings of wind and weather, tide and wave. They handle their boats with care and skill.

Very few of the islanders can swim. They like to say that if you cannot swim, you'll be more careful on the sea, and that for the non-swimmer, death by drowning will be quicker and without a struggle.

In this passage from Synge's *Riders to the Sea* Old Maurya is lamenting for the children she has lost to the sea and expressing her conviction that her youngest son Bartley will now also be drowned. Her daughter Nora tries to console her.

NORA: Didn't the young priest say the Almighty God won't leave her destitute with no son living?

MAURYA (*in a low voice, but clearly*): It's little the like of him knows of the sea.... Bartley will be lost by now, and let you call in Eamon and make me a good coffin out of the white boards, for I won't live after them. I've had a husband, and a husband's father, and six sons in this house — six fine men, though it was a hard birth I had with every one of them and they coming to the world — and some of them were found and some of them were not found, but they're gone now the lot of them... There were Stephen and Shawn were lost in the great wind, and found after in the Bay of Gregory of the Golden Mouth, and carried up the two of them on one plank, and in by that door.

CATHLEEN (*in a whisper*): There's someone after crying out by the seashore.

MAURYA (*continues without hearing anything*): There was Sheamus and his father, and his own father again, were lost in a dark night, and not a stick or sign was seen of them when the sun went up. There was Patch after was drowned out of a curragh that turned over. I was sitting here with Bartley, and he a baby lying on my two knees, and I seen two women, and three women, and four women coming in, and they crossing themselves and not saying a word. I looked out then, and there were men coming after them, and they holding a thing in the half of a red sail, and water dripping out of it   it was a dry day, Nora — and leaving a track to the door.

THE CLEGGAN DISASTER

In 1927, twenty-five fishermen from the Cleggan area of Co.
Galway were drowned in a storm while fishing. This excerpt is
from Richard Murphy's long poem *The Cleggan Disaster.*

Whose is that hulk on the shingle
The boatwright's son repairs
Though she has not been fishing
For thirty-four years
Since she rode the disaster?
The oars were turned into rafters
For a roof stripped by a gale.
Moss has grown on her keel.

Where are the red-haired women
Chattering along the piers
Who gutted millions of mackerel
And baited the spillet hooks
With mussels and lug-worms?
All the hurtful hours
Thinking the boats were coming
They hold against those years.

Where are the barefoot children
With brown toes in the ashes
Who went to the well for water,
Picked winkles on the beach
And gathered sea-rods in winter?
The lime is green on the stone
Which they once kept white-washed.
In summer nettles return.

Where are the dances in houses
With porter and cakes in the room,
The reddled faces of fiddlers
Sawing out jigs and reels,
The flickering eyes of neighbours?
The thatch which was neatly bordered
By a fringe of sea-stones
Has now caved in.

Why does she stand at the curtains
Combing her seal-grey hair
And uttering bitter opinions
On land-work and sea-fear,
Drownings and famines?
When will her son say,
"Forget about the disaster,
We're mounting nets today!"

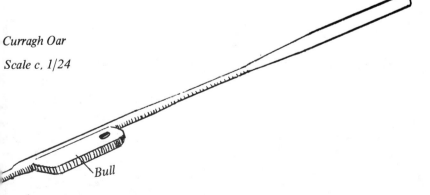

Curragh Oar

Scale c. 1/24

Bull

THE SEA

I am patient, repetitive, multi-voiced,
Yet few hear me
And fewer still trouble to understand

Why, for example, I caress
And hammer the land.
I do not brag of my depths

Or my currents, I do not
Boast of my moods or my colours
Or my breath in your thought.

In time I surrender my drowned,
My appetite speaks for itself,
I could swallow all you have found

And open for more,
My green tongues licking the shores
Of the world

Like starved beasts reaching for
Who will not understand
When I rage and roar

When I bellow and threaten
I am obeying a law
Observing a discipline.

This is the rhythm
I live.
This is the reason I move

In hunger and skill
To give you the pick of my creat
This is why I am willing to kill,

Chill every created nerve.
You have made me a savage mast
Because I know how to serve.

Brendan Kennelly

BOATS

The curragh is an open canoe which is ideally suited to
nditions in the Aran Islands. She can ride successfully in almost
y sea and weather conditions; she slips rapidly over the surface
calm water but she can just as easily cope with the mountainous
hite crested waves of a stormy sea. The curragh needs neither
er nor harbour as she can be run ashore on any smooth patch
sand or gravel. Three men can hoist an upturned curragh onto
eir shoulders without undue strain and lay her on a stone
radle' above high tide mark until she will be needed again. A
rragh being transported in this way looks, from above, like a
gantic six-legged beetle.

The islanders are dependent on the curragh for the transporting
their everyday needs. People, animals and goods are all carted
the curragh and she is invaluable in those islands which do not
ve a harbour where steamer or hooker can safely land.

The ancient curraghs were made from the skins of animals,
rticularly cowhides, but more recently the materials needed
ve been brought in from the mainland. For the Aran Islands
rragh a light wooden frame is first constructed using (in the
ree-man model) thirty ribs spaced 14 centimetres apart. The
s are sawn laths, the dimensions of which are 4 cm. by 1.5 cm.
e gunwhales are fashioned from wood also and are about 7 cm.
de by 5 cms. deep. Heavy canvas is then stretched over this
ame and securely fastened. Finally, the boat receives several
ats of tar to make her waterproof. When complete the three-
an Aran curragh is 6 metres long and a four-man boat may
easure up to 8 metres. The beam, or breadth of the boat at the
ntre, varies from about 8 metres and its depth is about 1 metre.
a curragh is handled with care and promptly repaired it should
ve at least eight years of service. A hole in the canvas of the boat
easily repaired by its owner. The tar around the hole is melted.
piece of canvas is then placed over it and then tarred over
veral times until it is almost invisible. Although the Aran curragh
now constructed from modern materials the primitive design is
ill retained. It has been tried and proved over the centuries and
ill gives good service to the islanders.

ROWING A CURRAGH

A curragh has no keel, and so depends on the skill of h
oarsmen and on ballast for her grip on the water. Ballast is ext
weight carried in a boat to make her 'sit' safely in the water and
Aran it takes the form of carefully chosen round boulders.

The curragh is rowed with long, narrow, bladeless oars. Eac
oarsman rows with two of these oars, the hole in the "Bull" c
the oar sitting over a wooden tholepin or peg which stanc
vertically on the gunwhale of the boat. This allows the oar to pivc
back and forth but it cannot be swept away, if, for any reason, th
oarsman should let loose his grip. Rowing and steering a currag
require great skill. The oarsman must also be a good judge of th
opportune moment for launching and beaching the boat.
mistake could result in the boat being smashed or swamped and i
her crew being lost.

Sometimes a simple sail is rigged in a curragh and an oar
extended over the stern to act as a steer.

John Millington Synge described the launching of a curragh

'In bad weather, four men will often stand for nearly an hou
at the top of the slip with a curragh in their hands, watching
point of rock towards the south where they can see the strengt
of the waves that are coming in.

The instant a break is seen, they swoop down to the sur
launch their curragh, and pull out to sea with incredible speec
Coming to land is attended with the same difficulty, and, if th
moment is badly chosen, they are likely to be washed sideway
and swamped among the rocks.'

But bringing a curragh to land could be even more dangerou
as he soon discovered.

'Late this evening, I saw a three-oared curragh with two ol
women in her besides the rowers, landing at the slip through
heavy roll. They were coming from Inisheer, and they rowed u
quickly enough till they were within a few yards of the sur
line, where they spun round and waited with the prow toward
the sea, while wave after wave passed underneath them and brok
on the remains of the slip. Five minutes passed; ten minutes; and
still they waited with the oars just paddling in the water, and thei
heads turned over their shoulders.

I was beginning to think they would have to give up and row

The Aran Island Curragh

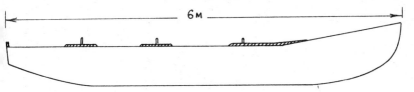

ELEVATION

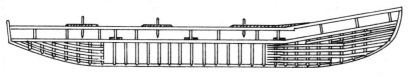

A.Monnelly   ELEVATION   (without canvas, laths not completed)

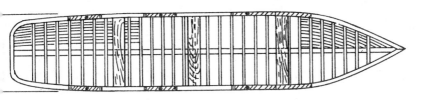

A.Monnelly   PLAN   (laths not completed)

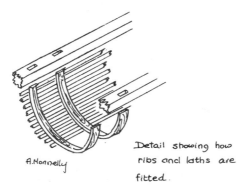

A.Monnelly

Detail showing how
ribs and laths are
fitted.

Hookers at Kilronan pier around 1890. Their curved side planks and single stout mast are distinctive. On the left is a large two masted sailing trawler of the kind used in Aran waters by Arklow fishermen. A steamer has moored in the bay as it cannot approach the pier at low tide. Row boats are busy ferrying visitors to and from the ship.

round to the lee side of the island, when the curragh seemed suddenly to turn into a living thing. The prow was again towards the slip, leaping and hurling itself through the spray. Before it touched, the man in the bow wheeled round, two white legs came out over the prow like the flash of a sword, and before the next wave arrived he had dragged the curragh out of danger.

This sudden and united action in men without discipline shows well the education that the waves have given them. When the curragh was in safety the two old women were carried up through the surf and slippery seaweed on the backs of their sons.

In this broken weather a curragh cannot go out without danger, yet accidents are rare and seem to be nearly always caused by drink. Since I was here last year four men have been drowned on their way home from the large island. First a curragh belonging to the south island which put off with two men in her heavy with drink, came to shore here the next evening dry and uninjured, with the sail half set and no one in her.

More recently a curragh from this island with three men, who were the worse for drink was upset on its way home. The steamer was not far off, and saved two of the men, but could not reach the third."

THE GALWAY HOOKER

A large wooden hulled boat, the Galway Bay Hooker, sometimes called the Connemara Hooker, is used by the mainlanders for fishing, shark hunting and carting turf to the islands. They are single masted sailing boats which are easily recognisable by their dark brown sails and high, tarred hull.

THE SEA

*Look you out
northeastwards
Over mighty ocean,
Teeming with sea-life;
Home of seals,
Sporting, splendid,
Its tide has reached
fullness.*

(Medieval Irish Lyric)

A group of Kilronan fishermen dressed in the traditional bawneens and pampooties. A two-masted sailing trawler is berthed at the pier. In the bay an ice hulk is anchored to supply ice for keeping trawl fish fresh until it can be shipped to market in Galway. Straw Island and its lighthouse are in the background.

FISHING

Over thirty varieties of fish are found in the waters around the Aran Islands and the islanders fish for many of these at various times of the year. The fishermen use different types of gear to land the particular species.

DRIFT NETS

Drift nets are nets which float in an upright position near the surface creating a 'wall' into which mackerel and herring blindly swim. 'Drifting' is carried on at night when the nets are invisible to the fish and the shoals rise nearer to the surface. The islanders use curraghs for this work but, since 1892, Aranmen have fished on large wooden, sailing drifters which visit Galway Bay for the rich spring and autumn mackerel fishery. These boats, from the east coast of Ireland, land large catches which are salted down for export to America. This large scale 'curing' operation provides valuable seasonal employment for women.

LONG LINES

Long lines are used to catch those fish which live on, or near, the sea bed and which include 'round' fish like cod, ling and pollock, and 'flat' fish like plaice, sole and turbot. The long lines, as the name suggests are lines of about 200–300 metres in length which have 100 or more hooks attached. The hooks are baited with slugs or salt fish and the long line is anchored in a suitable location and left out overnight. Two buoys, one at either end, mark the place where the line has been set.

POTS

Lines of pots are used to catch shellfish such as lobster and crayfish. The pots for catching lobster are made from willow, and those for crayfish are made from thin laths. They are weighted with stones and have baits fixed inside an opening. Several pots are attached at intervals to a rope and they are lowered to the sea bed. A buoy or float at either end marks the spot.

The pots may be hauled and rebaited several times in the course

The most important species of fish found in Aran waters are:

MACKEREL
(ronnach)

POLLOCK
White/Black
(pollóg)

HADDOCK
(cadóg)

HERRING
(scadán)

LING
(langa)

COD OR
CODLING
(trosc)

TURBOT
(turbard)

PLAICE
(leathóg)

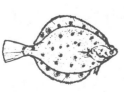

of the day. The lobsters which have crawled in through the narrow basket shaped entrance are trapped and cannot climb out again. They are stored in a floating crate made of wood, through which the sea freely passes and they are marketed weekly or when a sufficient quantity has been gathered. This type of fishing can only be conducted in the very calmest summer weather as it involves working close to cliffs and submerged reefs. The catch is valuable and a good season can boost the finances of island families but the risks involved are considerable.

HAND LINES

Hand lines are used occasionally to catch mackerel, pollock and bass. They may be worked from a curragh but fishing from the cliff tops is quite common. The islander squats at the very edge of a sheer drop, up to one hundred metres above the ocean surface, and casts and hauls his line from this dangerous position.

'CURING' FISH

Mackerel, herring, cod, pollock and ling which are not sold immediately must be 'cured' for winter use. The cleaned and gutted fish may be packed into a barrel containing a pickle made of coarse salt and fresh water. Mackerel and herring are usually cured in this way. Cod and ling may be pickled lightly in a barrel for a short period, then hung on the rafters or spread on a flat stone to dry. When 'cured' the fish will keep for a considerable time and will retain their food value and their flavour.

SHARKS

In the past sharks were more often found in the waters around Aran. They were hunted and killed with harpoons by the islanders who would cut out the liver and discard the body of the shark. The liver of a single shark could, when boiled, produce up to 900 litres of oil which is used for domestic lighting.

BELIEFS AND CUSTOMS

Fishing is an occupation which offers varying rewards. In a sense the fisherman takes his life in his hands each time he launches a curragh. Safety at sea and a good catch can never be

uaranteed. Therefore the fisherman takes precautions to avoid
lamaging his luck, as he sees it.

If the fisherman, on the way to the shore, meets a red-haired
r barefoot woman, it is regarded as a bad omen for the day's
vork. Meeting a hare, a rabbit, a priest or a fox is also regarded
s being unlucky and, while at sea, the fishermen avoid mentioning
priest, or a pig or a weasel. Three men of the same name must
ot fish together nor should anybody smoke while at his work.
Vhen at home, a fisherman is careful not to throw a fish bone in
he fire.

Boats never put to sea on a Saturday night nor do they fish
n St. Martin's Day, the 11th of November, or the eve of
Michaelmas which falls on the 28th September. Nets are lowered
nto the water in the name of God, Mary and St. Peter and the
osary is often recited at midnight while the men wait to haul.

A fleet of iron masted trawlers and single masted hookers
at Kilronan around 1890.

the shore

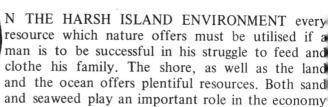

N THE HARSH ISLAND ENVIRONMENT every resource which nature offers must be utilised if a man is to be successful in his struggle to feed and clothe his family. The shore, as well as the land and the ocean offers plentiful resources. Both sand and seaweed play an important role in the economy of the islands.

FERTILISER

The only fertilisers available to the Aran farmer who wishes to improve his stony fields are sand and seaweed. The sand found on the Aran beaches has been created by the erosion of limestone rock. It is highly calcareous and is of benefit in growing potatoes. Certain kinds of seaweed can serve the same function and are hauled to the fields at seeding time, using a donkey and panniers.

KELP

Kelp is an iodine-rich substance which is produced by burning red seaweed. The islanders sell this to factories on the mainland where it is used in the making of chemicals and drugs. The red weed grows under water and is best gathered after the autumn and winter storms. Often the islanders must wade thigh deep in the icy water to cut the seaweed from submerged rocks so the work must be done on a calm day when tides are low. Knives and sickles attached to long handles are used for cutting the weed from the deeper water. This deep-water weed is prized, as it is entirely free of sand.

Sea-rods, which are the stalks of seaweeds, being stacked. They are exported for chemical processing. One of the main extracts is iodine.

The wet seaweed is carried up from the shore in panniers by donkey. It is hard, heavy work, as it takes more than 25 tonnes of weed to make one tonne of kelp and the work must be completed quickly while tides are favourable. If a family does not own a donkey they must carry the weed in baskets on their backs. Because the men are busy cutting the weed, women sometimes do this work wearing an animal hide on their back to protect their clothing.

When gathered, the weed is laid out to dry on walls and rocks and then piled up in ricks, not unlike haycocks, where it is left until early June. June is the usual time for burning the kelp. A kelp kiln, a low, rectangular stone trough, capable of holding about two tonnes of weed, is constructed for burning the dry seaweed. Firing must be done properly as the kelp may be ruined if not given enough time to 'run' or if fired for too long. As the weed begins to melt it is stirred with long iron rakes until it turns into a molten mass. When the firing is complete the kelp is left to cool in the kiln. After a few days the substance is as hard as limestone and has to be broken up with a sledge hammer before it is transported in curraghs to Kilronan. There it is tested for quality and the kelp-burner is paid. Later, the steamer will take it to the mainland.

Thomas O'Flaherty, an islander, writes about a conversation he had with one of his neighbours, Old Michael, when the old man was burning his kelp. The islanders have discovered that if they do not stir the kelp as it burns, it will emerge as a powder, equally rich in iodine, but much easier to manage and transport as it can be packed into bags.

' "And doesn't the kelp run at all now and don't you have to break it up with a sledge?"

"Damn the run,...: They say it's better to have her in small stones or in powder. We put her all in bags now. In your time there was no respect at all for the kelp that was in the bags. Everything is different now. We don't work as hard as we used to and though there is no money we live better than we ever did. We are eating meat now my boy!"

"How many tons are you going to have, Michael?" I asked.

"Now .... I wouldn't like to say anything rash, but if I don't send five tons over to Kilronan I hope I may not be alive a year from to-day. That kiln is twenty feet long if she is an inch. She is three feet wide and a foot and a half in height. I'll have to burn another one. That's not bad work for a year, and we planted a lot of potatoes. Of course I have the help, God bless them. But even so it's good work and I going on my seventy-five. And only for the bad reports we had all the year about the price I'd have another ton."

"You'll have the price of the turf anyhow, Michael."

"Faith I will and enough to buy five times as much as I need. If she doesn't test six pounds a ton at least may I be stricken dead if I ever make another ton."

"That's a rash threat, Michael," I said.

"Ah sure that's only talk," he laughed. "We have to be saying something. I'd be making kelp if I never got a penny for it through force of habit. *Sé an nádúr agam é.*"

And so I walked home up the shore from Poll na Luinge with the pleasant smell of the burning seaweed in my nostrils and the soothing poteen in my blood. What a great life it was, surely, burning kelp, fishing and planting potatoes in Aran.'

WRACK

The islands are self-sufficient in many of the essentials of life. A man may build a house and a boat and feed and clothe his family from the resources available to him locally. But he cannot provide timber or fuel as there are no trees on the island. Such items must be imported from the mainland and paid for in cash. Kelp and cattle may pay for the turf but timber, for house-building and other purposes, is almost beyond the financial means of the islanders.

Driftwood, washed up on the beaches and on the rock platforms which fringe the base of the cliffs, offers a solution to this problem. Stormy weather may bring a floating harvest of planks and spars but the islanders greet the appearance of wreckage with mixed feelings. They know that their good luck must certainly mean misfortune for other human beings.

Thomas O'Flaherty describes an expedition in which he joined his father and a group of other men to gather wrack.

'It was half ebb when we got to the Port of the Fort's Mouth. Old villagers who were too shaky to risk the tall cliffs prowled among the boulders picking up a plank here and there. Out in the mouth of the little bay planks were carried back and forth by the current. Now and then a barrel rolled over. What was in the barrels? Rum, oil, grease, tar?   We would know later.

My father could hardly restrain the men from picking up stray pieces of timber. "Wait until we get to the Blind Sound," he said. "We'll gather more in one hour there than we would gather here all day."

We walked along the cliff peering at the sea. The surface of the water was unbroken as the wind had died down. Long, lazy swells rolled in from the deep, crested, and broke on the shallows. Every once in a while an exclamation would burst from one of the men:

"Look south-westerly from you, where the seagulls are! There's a whole ship load of timber there."

Suddenly I wondered what happened to the sailors who manned the wrecked vessel and I shuddered as I visualised myself going down to death in that terrible sea. Groups of men from Gort na gCapall and from Kilmurvey had picked choice spots along the cliff at and near the Blind Sound. Our advance agents had a good place. The limestone rock on the cliff's edge was smooth and would not fray the cable. The cliff was straight until within five fathoms of the bottom. There were no jutting rocks on the face of the cliff to catch the planks as they were being hauled up.

Nobody had gone down yet as there was very little of the shore at the bottom dry. Planks were piled among the rocks. Sometimes a sea would drive a plank end on against a rock and split it. Men often had their legs broken in similar situations. We were all watching the precious timber below. Hundreds of planks were suddenly left dry by a receding wave.

"Time to go down," said Bartley Pat. The cable was lashed around his body. He stood on the top of the cliff and took off his cap.

"Now, in the name of the Father, Son and Holy Ghost," he said. He turned his back to the sea, his face to the land and disappeared over the edge.

Little Jimmy was watching the descent from a vantage point and giving us directions with his hands. We lowered gradually. When Bartley had touched bottom we hauled up the rope and let the other two men down. All along the cliff men were descending, dancing in and out, steering themselves with one hand, the other holding on to the rope, striking the cliff with the sole of one foot swinging gracefully out and in until they landed at the bottom. It was a feat that called for daring and experience.

Soon we were hauling up planks and hiding them in the scalps. The coastguards would lay claim to the wrack in the name of the

The curraghs land the goods at Inishmaan.

King of England if they found it.

Furiously we worked. The men at the bottom kept sending up planks until the tide came in again. Two of them were hauled up. Then it was Bartley Pat's turn. Little Jimmy raised his hand.

We started to haul. Nobody was watching Jimmy. We were thinking about the timber.

Little Jimmy was frantically signalling us to lower. We payed out the rope slowly. "Very slowly," he signalled. We did not know what was the matter until we brought Bartley to the top.

"I thought I was as dead as a pickled herring," he chuckled. "Little Jimmy thought I gave him the signal to haul while I only wanted more rope. I only had one leg in the coil when ye hauled and I was hoisted half way up the cliff by the ankle."

"You weren't born to be hanged by the legs," my father remarked.

We put in the best part of a week gathering wrack. After the timber was safely stored away in deep clefts and caves, the coast-guards visited the village and asked if any timber was washed ashore at the Point of the Fort's Mouth. The villagers advised them that there wasn't a stick to be seen there. The coastguards thanked them for the information and returned to their quarters in Kilronan.'

the home

THE TRADITIONAL ARAN HOUSE TYPE is well suited to the windswept, stormy conditions found on the western seaboard. It is a long, low, single-storied cottage with a thatched roof. Though the size of these houses may vary considerably they all share the same basic design. They are rectangular structures with thick stone walls mortared with clay or cement. Windows and doors are set in the long side of the house rather than in the gables. The roof is steeply pitched and its weight is borne upon the walls. All have an open hearth at floor level, with a chimney protruding through the roof ridge. The walls are usually covered with whitewash which is renewed every year. There are of course other house types to be found on the islands, such as the two storied slate-roofed houses which can be seen in Kilronan and some of the larger settlements. The traditional house, however, is well adapted to climatic conditions on the island and it has the added advantage of using locally available materials. Windows are small, and are deeply set in the walls. In the past some cottages had no windows at all as rent was often calculated by the landlord on the basis of the number and size of the windows. In any case, small windows are suited to local conditions, and the combination of thick stone walls, thatched roof, and small windows with even smaller panes of glass, keeps the house warm in winter, and pleasantly cool in summer.

Doors are set in the front and back of the house. One or other almost always remains open by day, both as a means of ventilating the house and as a sign of welcome to callers. The front door may

Above — Aran houses. Thick dry stone walls make the house snug in winter and cool in summer. The roof thatch is criss-crossed with sugans or grass ropes, which are tied down as a protection against the storms of winter. The outhouse on the right is a more basic structure. It is of dry stone construction, that is, no mortar has been used in the walls, a building technique practised on Aran for several thousand years. The gable 'steps up' to the roof. ridge in this type of building.

Below — Ground plans of two variations on the basic house type which are frequently found in coastal locations. One has the hearth set in the gable wall. In the other the hearth is set into the dividing wall in the centre of the house. In both cases the rooms occupy the full width of the house and open into one another.

gable hearth type   **central hearth type**

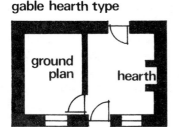

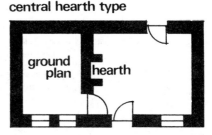

be divided in two horizontally and on windy days only the top half is opened to prevent draughts. This half-door arrangement is useful for keeping young children indoors and for preventing farm animals from entering. It also provides a comfortable arm rest for the woman of the house when she leans out and chats with her neighbours.

There are many traditional beliefs regarding the back door which are still respected. It is considered unlucky for a stranger to leave the house by the back door. When a death has occurred in the house it is customary to carry the coffin out through the back door.

BUILDING A HOUSE

Sometimes, when a young man marries he may leave the family home and build his own house with the help of friends and neighbours. The site for a house is carefully chosen, taking account of slope, shelter and distance from other dwellings. The work of building the house is carried on in a cheerful atmosphere. When completed the owner invites his helpers and neighbours to a house warming *céili* which is an occasion for general celebration.

THATCHING

When the building is finished and the roof rafters have been positioned the thatcher is called in. The thatcher is a respected craftsman who is much in demand in spring, summer and autumn. To keep the roof fully waterproofed the thatch must be repaired each year and the whole thatch must be completely renewed after seven or eight years.

The Aran houses have a gable roof which means that high gable walls rise up to the roof ridge. This arrangement is ideal for windy coastal areas. Elsewhere in Ireland traditional houses have a four sided or "hip roof" where the thatch slopes down at the sides to meet the gable at the same height as it meets the front wall.

Thatching is a reasonably cheap way of roofing a house as the materials used are available locally. It provides a warm, dry roof in winter, and, when secured properly with ropes and weights, it can withstand the fierce Atlantic gales.

It must be repaired and renewed often however, and there is always a risk that a stray spark can set the whole roof on fire.

Tomás Ó Crohan, who was born and lived his life on the Blasket

A fine example of the traditional Irish long house on Aran. Deep set
windows, whitewashed stone walls and securely roped thatch are all features
which reflect the influence of the environment and the use of local materials.

THE THATCHER

Bespoke for weeks, he turned up some morning
Unexpectedly, his bicycle slung
With a light ladder and a bag of knives.
He eyed the old rigging, poked at the eaves.

Opened and handled sheaves of lashed wheat-straw.
Next, the bundled rods: hazel and willow
Were flicked for weight, twisted in case they'd snap.
It seemed he spent the morning warming up:

Then fixed the ladder, laid out well honed blades
And snipped at straw and sharpened ends of rods
That, bent in two, made a white-pronged staple
For pinning down his world, handful by handful.

Couchant for days on sods above the rafters
He shaved and flushed the butts, stitched all together
Into a sloped honeycomb, a stubble patch,
And left them gaping at his Midas touch.

Seamus Heaney

Islands, Co. Kerry, describes other problems which a thatche roof can cause:

"The thatch would have been all right if the hens would on have let it alone, but they wouldn't. As soon as the rushes bega to decay, and worms could be found in them, a man with a gu couldn't have kept the hens away from scratching and nestir there. Then the drips would begin, and a dirty drip it was too, fe there was too much soot mixed with it. The hens nested so dee in the thatch that the women often lost them, for a hen wouldn even answer the call to food when she was broody. The litt lasses very often brought a hatful or a capful of eggs down fro the houses. The children made a mess of the thatch too, alwa hunting for eggs. It was as good as a day at Puck Fair to listen t two of the women whose houses adjoined, quarrelling with on another about the ownership of the eggs."

DÍON SÚGÁN – ROPED THATCH

As we have seen, the usual material for thatching in Aran rye-straw. It is tough and hardy and has quite a long life. Befor a roof is thatched, a thin layer of rough grass (or, in areas mor fertile than Aran, heather sods) is fixed over the roof timber This forms a sound base for the thatch.

The thatcher first spreads a layer of straw, about 10 cm. thick along the eaves at the base of the roof. Then he spreads anothe layer above this, overlapping the first; and so on until he reache the roof-ridge.

When he has finished one side, the thatcher starts at the bottor of the other side, and works his way up the ridge again. Finally, quantity of straw is spread evenly over the ridge.

The new roof is now ready to be secured. The thatcher stretche long pieces of grass rope *súgán* over the roof ridge at interva of about 30 cms. These are fixed to wooden or stone pegs set int the wall beneath the eaves. Sometimes, where there are no peg the rope is tied to heavy stones which hang over the eaves an weigh down the thatch. Other pieces of rope are then fixe crosswise, sometimes all over the thatch, sometimes just at th ridge and eaves, and fastened to pegs set into the gable walls.

The rope forms a heavy net over the thatch and keeps it i place. When the thatcher wants to renew the thatch, he firs removes the old rope. The rope is made by the people of the hous helped by friends and neighbours. Here, Synge describes how th

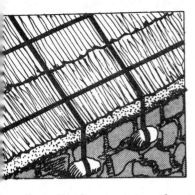

Roped Thatch, (in Irish Díon Súgán)

people twist the straw together to make the rope:

"In our own cottage the thatching — it is done every year — has just been carried out. The rope-twisting was done partly in the lane, partly in the kitchen when the weather was uncertain. Two men usually sit together at this work, one of them hammering the straw with a heavy block of wood, the other forming the rope, the main body of which is twisted by a boy or girl with a bent stick specially formed for this employment.

In wet weather, when the work must be done indoors, the person who is twisting recedes gradually out of the door, across the lane, and sometimes across a field or two beyond it. A great length is needed to form the close network which is spread over the thatch, as each piece measures about fifty yards. When this work is in progress in half the cottages of the village, the road has a curious look, and one has to pick one's steps through a maze of twisting ropes that pass from the dark doorways on either side into the fields.

When four or five immense balls of rope have been completed, a thatching party is arranged, and before dawn some morning they come down to the house, and the work is taken in hand with such energy that it is usually ended within the day.

Like all work that is done in common on the island, the thatching is regarded as a sort of festival. From the moment a roof is taken in hand there is a whirl of laughter and talk till it is ended, and, as the man whose house is being covered is a host instead of an employer, he lays himself out to please the men who work with him.

The day our own house was thatched the large table was taken into the kitchen from my room, and high teas were given every few hours. Most of the people who came along the road turned down into the kitchen for a few minutes, and the talking was incessant."

INSIDE THE COTTAGE

The centre of every Aran home is the hearth which is set a ground level in the stone flagged kitchen. The fire is kept aligh constantly, both in summer and in winter. At night, ashes ar piled over the burning sods to keep the embers glowing unt morning. The fire sits at floor level on iron rods with a shallo pit underneath into which the ashes can fall. A wide chimne breast juts out from the wall, creating a large recess on eithe side of the fire. Many hearths have a stone bench built into thi recess which provides a warm seat for an old or ailing membe of the family.

An iron 'crane' stands at one side with a jib extending ove the back of the fire. Several hooks hang from this and the woma of the house suspends the kettle and cast-iron cooking pots o them. Sods of turf are placed on the fire with iron tongs and th stone flags around the hearth are swept with a small bundle o twigs tied together for this purpose.

Many cottages have a *cleibhí,* a small square cubby hole, set i to the wall of the hearth. Pipes, tobacco, and perhaps tea, are kep in these, ready for use when required.

TURF

Though the islands have an extremely heavy rainfall, surfac water drains off quickly and percolates down through the man cracks in the limestone pavements. Peat has never had th opportunity to form on this dry surface and the islanders ar severely handicapped by the absence of bogs where they coul cut and 'save' their own fuel. All turf used on the islands has to b bought and hookers cross over from the Connemara mainlan with regular loads of 'saved' turf. As many as fifteen hooker may come on a particular day and the islanders unload the fue and pay for it, usually in cash, but sometimes by bartering a cal or bullock with the suppliers.

FURNITURE

Houses on Aran are small and some structures basically consis of a single room. Space is precious and the furniture strictl functional — small chairs, a table, a dresser, beds, a wooden ches for storage and a long bench-seat which stands against the back wall.

Tomás Ó Crohan of the Blasket Islands writes about the house he grew up in, typical of the island dwellings of the 1870's and 880's:

"The tables used in the little houses were rather like a kneading trough — a board with a raised frame round it to keep in the potatoes or anything else they put on them, and a stand of tripod shape that could be folded up so that the stand and the kneading trough could be hung up on the wall till they were needed.

We had bowls and plates in every house, wooden mugs, a chair or two, and a few stools. The chairs had seats of twisted rope made of hay or straw. There was a pot-rack of iron in every house, and still is, to hang things on over the fire, and there was a pair of tongs of some sort or other on the hearth.

They have cups and saucers in every house now and a full dresser, making a fine show."

The sleeping area, in such a house, is usually not large enough for the whole family, so some members may sleep in the kitchen in a settle-bed — a simple bedstead of wood which can be doubled up to form a high backed bench by day. In other instances, a family may keep a bed upright against the kitchen wall and tip it down when it is needed at night.

LIGHTING

Candles and oil lamps, supplied from the mainland, provide light for the houses at night. When sharks were more plentiful, their oil, or that of seals or even that of fish such as scad and pollock, was burned with a straw or rush wick in a home-made lamp called a cresset.

Tomás Ó Crohan describes these lamps as used on his island around 1880:

"The cresset was a little vessel, shaped like a boat or canoe, with one or two pointed ends, three or four feet to it, and a little handle or grip sticking out of its side — the whole thing about eight or ten inches long. The fish or seal oil was put into it, the reed or wick was dipped in the oil and passed over the pointed end of the cresset, and as it burnt away, it was pushed out. The pith of the rush formed the wick, and often they used a soft twine of cotton or linen for it. They would often use a large shell instead of a cresset for a light. I don't remember at what date paraffin came

in. A fragment of turf or a chip of bog-deal was the older fashion
I used to hear them say."

FOOD AND DRINK

Potatoes are an essential part of an Aran family's diet. They are
eaten in quantity for 'dinner', the main meal, taken at mid-day
in most homes. They are boiled in their jackets in a large round
bottomed iron pot which is suspended from a hook over the fire.
When cooking is complete the pot is stood on its cast iron legs at
one side of the fire and the potatoes transferred to a plate, or, in
some cases, a shallow wicker basket. Potatoes are flavoured with
salt and butter and milk is usually consumed with the meal. Other
food such as salt fish, may be cooked or stewed with the potatoes.

Fresh meat is usually eaten only when a farmer kills one of his
sheep or pigs. On such occasions he will share the meat with
neighbouring families. Bacon, which is home cured, is the most
frequently eaten meat. At certain festive times of the year, such
as Christmas and Easter, a family may eat one of their chickens
or geese.

A limited variety of vegetables is produced for home
consumption. Families may grow some onions and cabbage in a
small 'garden' near the dwelling house. Cabbage is the most
popular vegetable and is frequently eaten with boiled bacon. It
may also be mixed with potatoes and onions in a dish called
'colcannon'.

Colcannon should correctly be made with kale, but is more
often made with cabbage. A plain gold ring, a sixpence, a thimble
or a button are often put into the mixture. The ring means you
will be married within a year; the sixpence denotes wealth, the
thimble a spinster and the button a bachelor. The following is a
common recipe:

1 lb. each of kale or cabbage, and potatoes, cooked separately
2 small leeks or green onion tops
1 cup milk or cream
4 oz. (½ cup) approx. butter
Salt, pepper and a pinch of mace

Have the kale or cabbage cooked, warm and well chopped up
while the potatoes are cooking. Chop up the leeks or onion tops

while the potatoes are cooking. Chop up the leeks or onion tops, green as well as white, and simmer them in milk or cream to just cover, until they are soft. Drain the potatoes, season and beat them well; then add the cooked leeks and milk.

Finally blend in the kale, beating until it is a pale green fluff. Do this over a low flame and pile it into a deep warmed dish. Make a well in the centre and pour in enough melted butter to fill up the cavity. The vegetables are served with spoonfuls of the melted butter. Any leftovers can be fried in hot bacon fat until crisp and brown on both sides.

White and brown wheaten flour, and yellow maize flour, must be delivered from the mainland. Bread dough is mixed using skimmed milk and bread soda and the bread is baked in a pot-oven. The pot-oven is a straight-sided, flat-bottomed iron pot which sits on a bed of embers at the side of the fire. The dough is placed in the pot, and the iron lid covered with glowing turf-sparks. The dough is thus heated from both bottom and top and is baked slowly and evenly. The pot-oven can also be used for roasting fresh meat or fresh fish such as ray.

Milk and tea are drunk in every home. Buttermilk left over after churning, is a refreshing, if sharp, occasional drink. Water for tea is boiled in a heavy iron kettle suspended from the fire crane. It is customary to keep a kettle "on the boil" in between mealtimes so that tea can be brewed for anyone who calls.

CLOTHES

The men wear trousers and waistcoats of homespun tweed, grey or light-brown in colour. Under the waistcoat they wear a woollen sweater or 'gansey' which may be a natural off-white colour or, sometimes, dyed dark blue. A brightly coloured belt called a crios may be tied around the waist and knitted socks and hand-made cowhide slippers called 'pampooties' are the usual footwear. An Aran man wears a knitted cap, seldom removed except at church and at mealtimes.

Women normally wear calf-length red or dark hand-woven skirts and knitted sweaters and they don headscarves or brightly coloured shawls when going out-of-doors. Like the men they wear pampooties and black woollen stockings.

Both boys and girls wear long dark coloured petticoats of wool, even when they have commenced school, lowering the hem as they grow. Later they wear a scaled down version of the adult dress. They go barefoot in summer.

SPINNING AND WEAVING

Wool is the principal material used by the island women in th
making of the family's clothing. Their own sheep supply most c
the wool which is spun in the home and sent to the local weave
who produces the cloth on a hand loom. From this cloth trouser
waistcoats and skirts are made, often by a travelling tailor wh
lives with each family while completing their order.

In this passage a visitor talks to an island woman who is engage
in spinning wool for her family's clothing:

'Passing the open door of a cottage one afternoon and catchir
a glimpse of a spinning wheel turning merrily, I paused for
moment to watch. The woman of the house, looking up, saw m
and invited me in.

I felt as if I had slipped right into the middle of an old story as
sat down on a low stool by the fire. The spinning wheel, mounte
on a low stand, dominated the small kitchen, and on the floc
beside it was a heap of fleecy wool in soft, loose strands.

Taking a strand of wool, the woman held it beside the end c
spun wool on the bobbin, then with her other hand she bega
turning the wheel.

"Whirr," away it went, and "birr" sang the shuttle merrily
while in and out she pulled the thread like elastic, bent down fc
another strand, and "whirr" it went again.

" 'Tis in a hurry I am," she told me, "to get it spun the way th
weaver can be making a bit of flannel for me."

"You have a weaver on the island?" I asked.

"Oh, faith and we have, he lives up beyond there." *Birr* sar
the shuttle.

"Would you like to be trying a hand at it yourself?" she askec
"Let you hold it like that," she showed me, as I took a strand c
fleece and began to turn the wheel.

The thread broke. She mended it, and I tried again. This tim
the wool flew into a tangled mess on the shuttle, much to th
amusement of the two children who had just come in from schoo

"I'll make it all right," their mother said comfortingly, and
stood by like a little girl learning knitting, who has handed a mes
of dropped stitches to her mother to be picked up.

"I'm afraid now it is the sack you would be getting and yo
trying to spin," she said, as she took it from me and deftly spu

Wool from the Aran sheep drying, having been washed and carded. The housewife will spin the wool into yarn which a local weaver will weave into cloth. The housewife, or a travelling tailor, will make the family's clothes from this cloth.

A spinning wheel used in island homes to make woollen yarn and knitting wool. In the background is the open dresser and delph, typical furniture of the Aran kitchen. In the left background is a large wooden chest used as a dry store for flour and oatmeal.

out the tangle.

When the bobbin was full, she brought over a ball of wool fit for a giantess to knit with, nearly seven pounds she said it weighed. It filled her whole wide red petticoat lap as she sat down and wound on the newly-spun thread, while a little girl held the bobbin.

When spun it looked a dirty greyish colour, but when washed she told me it comes up "white as the waves and them breaking."

Then she showed me another gigantic ball, this time of dark brown wool, the natural colour of the fleece from the dark sheep.

"Them two together makes a nice bit of cloth; wait a minute now and I'll show you a bit."

She brought over one of the sleeveless coats which the Aran men wear over their knitted jerseys. It was navy blue at the back, and this brown and white tweed in the front.

"It is how the women are the tailors on this island," she said; "we make everything, even the trousers."

"Then it is all home industry, right from the sheep-rearing to the clothesmaking?"

"All except the carding. We send the wool to Galway the way they would be carding it for us. The old women used to do that themselves, too, but it was heavy work surely, and half the night the poor things would be busy at it. It comes lighter on us now, though faith and it is hard enough."

"And what about the jerseys, do you knit them yourselves?" — for I had already admired the work of many of them — beautifully knitted they are, in elaborate patterns of ropes and trailing sprays.

"Faith and we do, every one of them; and dye the wool ourselves, too, with indigo dye, the stuff that would turn you out of the kitchen with the smell that's in it. And it is several days it must stay there in the pot; but when 'tis done, sure heaven and earth would be unable to move the colour that would be in it. Though indeed there is many would rather use the new dyes now, for it is a lot easier they are. But they are not near as good. With a dropeen of rain on them the dye comes off, and it is blue you would be underneath, and I'm thinking that can't be good for anyone, surely."

"And what about the red petticoats; how do you dye them?" I asked.

"Oh, it is the same way with them. It used to be all the old madder dye, but now it is the cheap red dyes they are getting from Galway, and I am thinking it is a pity. Ah, sure the whole world is changing; I don't know what is coming over things at all."

She, too, like everyone else, complained of the wet turf. The fire, instead of burning with a red glow, was all smouldering smoke, much of which came puffing out in clouds into the kitchen. Days and months of turf smoke had stained the white-washed chimney-piece a rich tobacco brown, and mellowed the old rafters. Above the chimney hung two bunches of cow-hide cut into squares ready to make pampooties.

Reluctantly I said good-bye, for I had stayed a long time fascinated by the whirr of the wheel and the talk of the woman as she turned it.'

KNITTING

Whereas the women of the islands have knitted their families' sweaters and stockings for centuries, the knitting of the 'Aran' sweater, with its intricate patterns of stitching was introduced to the islands only after the famine, as a means of creating cash employment. The 'sculptured' ornate sweaters quickly became part of every islander's clothing, and each family acquired its own distinctive combination of stitches. The patterns of the sweaters and stockings have been used to identify bodies recovered from the sea. The Aran women are remarkably proficient at this 'traditional' style of knitting and, working from memory, can rapidly create lines of stitches in a myriad of changing sequences.

THE CRIOS

Weaving the brightly coloured tie-belts is another distinctive craft practised by the islanders. The weaver makes a skein from lengths of different coloured wool. He holds the skein taut by placing one looped end around his neck and passing his foot through the other. Shuttle-like his hand is passed in and out through the strands, trailing coloured wools, and creating a variety of radiant designs. When the weaving of the crios is finished, the strands of wool at either end are plaited into long tassles. The wearer winds the crios several times round his waist and knots the ends together.

PAMPOOTIES

Pampooties are the light cowskin footwear of the Aran Islanders.

The cow hide is cleaned and hung on the kitchen wall or on the rafters until required. J. M. Synge was given a pair of these shoes by the family he lodged with, and had to learn how to walk in them. Here is his account of the incident:

'Michael walks so fast when I am out with him that I cannot pick my steps, and the sharp-edged fossils which abound in the limestone have cut my shoes to pieces.

The family held a consultation on them last night, and in the end it was decided to make me a pair of pampooties, which I have been wearing today among the rocks.

They consist simply of a piece of raw cowskin, with the hair outside, laced over the toe and round the heel with two ends of fishing-line that work round and are tied above the instep.

In the evening, when they are taken off, they are placed in a basin of water, as the rough hide cuts the foot and stocking if it is allowed to harden. For the same reason the people often step into the surf during the day, so that their feet are continually moist.

At first I threw my weight upon my heels, as one does naturally in a boot, and was a good deal bruised, but after a few hours I learned the natural walk of man, and could follow my guide in any portion of the island.

In one district below the cliffs, towards the north, one goes for nearly a mile jumping from one rock to another without a single ordinary step and here I realized that toes have a natural use, for I found myself jumping towards any tiny crevice in the rock before me, and clinging with an eager grip in which all the muscles of my feet ached from their exertion.'

BASKET-MAKING

Basket making is yet another of the crafts with which the islander must supply his everyday needs. Panniers for the donkey's back, storage baskets for turf and potatoes, dish-baskets for cooked potatoes and 'spillet' baskets for the fisherman's long lines are all made from the willow shoots, known locally as 'sally' which are grown in little groves about the island.

Basket making is a traditional craft which makes use of local material. The 'sallies', or willow rods, are grown in damp hollows around the islands. Baskets are used for carrying potatoes and turf, as a 'reel' for long-lines and as panniers for donkeys and horses.

Uprights are planted in the ground and a 'wall' is created by weaving lighter rods in and out between these uprights. The basket may be deep or shallow, rectangular, circular, or semi-circular, and trimmed with one or more handles depending on its function.

special occasions

CÉILÍ IS A GATHERING OF NEIGHBOURS and relatives for an evening's enjoyment and it usually involves music, dancing and story-telling as well as eating and drinking. The occasion for holding a ceílí may be a wedding in the family, the return of an emigrant or simply the celebration of a festive time of the year. The ceílí is held in the kitchen and adjoining room of the cottage. A barrel of stout is set up in the corner of the kitchen and one man is delegated to 'pull' the drink for the evening. Whiskey may also be provided, particularly for the old men who sit about the fire reminiscing on their young days. Poteen, illicit spirit distilled from grain, may be imported from the Connemara mainland for the occasion. The older women congregate in the room beside the kitchen where they enjoy a quiet chat while keeping an eye on the proceedings. Here, too, a table is set with food and the gathering is seated in shifts.

The musicians take their place in the corner of the kitchen and the man of the house ensures that their glasses are never empty. The fiddle and the accordion are the instruments most frequently played but the tin whistle, uileann pipes and fife or concert flute sometimes supply the music. A good musician is widely respected; his repertoire of tunes is a cherished hoard passed down through the bow strings of a long line of creative performers. Mainland musicians, particularly those from Co.Clare, are sometimes invited to play. In a crisis, when an instrumentalist can't be found, music is supplied by a lilter who reproduces the rhythms of the dance tune, varying a limited number of syllables with a suitable sound pattern.

SINGING

Solo singing is usually unaccompanied. Long lilting ballads tell of love and emigration and old sorrows. This style of singing, known as *sean nós,* involves difficult grace notes and flourishes. A good singer requires technical skill as well as the ability to interpret the emotions of the song. The audience listens attentively to the singer, interrupting at the end of a verse with a murmured word of encouragement, such as *Dia leat* or *Dia go deo leat.*

HOUSE-WALKING

A more frequent, and less formal, feature of social intercourse is the nightly visits of individuals to their neighbours' houses especially in the winter. The male members of the family engage in this while the women usually remain in their own homes. The men may sit and talk around the fire while smoking a pipe, or, in designated houses, play cards or listen to a *seanchaí.* They usually depart long before midnight. During the summer fishing season, if the sea is too rough for fishing, the men may congregate at the pier head or near the curragh stands and enjoy the sunshine as they talk.

MASS TIME

Sunday mornings offer an opportunity to both men and women to socialise and converse with their neighbours. People like to dress up in their best clothes and the women and girls bring out a special shawl kept for such occasions. The men and older boys walk to church on their own, the women and young children not usually appearing with husband or father. In church, men sit on the left hand side, women on the right, and after Mass, they leave the church grounds, or stand around chatting in groups, with members of their own sex.

MARRIAGE

Marriages on the islands are arranged with the general consent of the young couple and their parents. An uncle or adult friend of either family may conduct the bargaining which involves mutual agreement on the amount of the dowry which the bride's father will give her. The young couple have, of course, a considerable say in the matter and in most cases are well known to each other before any approach is made. Here, Tomás Ó Crohan, tells of how his family 'made' a match for him and he stresses the considerations which influenced their final choice.

'One night after I'd been out — and it was pretty late on in the night, too — whom should I find in the house when I came in but windy Diarmid, and his voice was going as loud as ever I'd heard it; he was getting at the old couple, explaining what an unhandy thing it'd be for them if they spent another year without a soul to help them — "and maybe two years," says he; "and I've got a proposal for you from the best girl that ever broke bread, the finest and the handsomest girl every way."

They didn't break off the talk after I came in, and we kept it up till you'd have thought that everybody in the house was in complete agreement; though the whole affair was to be gone into again, for all the advisers were not present. Be that as it may, Diarmid went out, and he could have trodden on a shell-less egg without breaking it. He fancied that the bargain was sealed.

My sister Maura, who had been in America and who had come back home and married again, heard that Diarmid the rake had been in our house with a match on his hands, and she came to see if there was any truth in the story. We told her how things stood, and she didn't like the idea at all; she made it plain to the old couple what a responsibility anyone was taking on himself if he didn't marry near home, but made an alliance with a family that lived a long way off and wouldn't be in a position to lend a hand on a rainy day.

She had herself marked down an excellent knowledgeable girl, whose people lived in the village, so that they could lend us a hand when we needed it, and she went on to explain the whole affair to us, like a woman reciting a litany, till she had the whole lot of us as tame as a cat.

She'd always had a great hankering after her first husband's people, and his brother's daughter it was that she'd marked down for us.'

Such marriages are generally successful when there is mutual goodwill and respect present. The wedding is an occasion for lavish hospitality and general celebration, the ceremony taking place shortly after the match is made. Early spring is the preferred season as it is not possible to have a marriage solemnised with nuptial Mass during Lent. Weddings may also take place in early summer but an autumn wedding is frowned upon. The islanders

like to say "what is bound in Autumn is loosed in the Spring"
Here is an account of a marriage ceremony and the *bain*
(wedding feast) which followed:

'Upon invitation of a cousin of a bride-to-be, we attended the
wedding of a young couple of Onaght, a village at the far end o
Inishmore. The ceremony took place in a chapel midway of the
island.

When we arrived the building was already filled with kneeling
friends, with a swarm of tufted-topped boys and young men
occupying the choir and leaning far forward so as to miss nothing
The bride and bridegroom knelt at the altar rail, with an attendan
at each side. The wedding ring reposed on the rail, on top of two
silver half-crowns, which seemed to be the fee.

The service was in Irish, except for the Latin ritual. It was al
very simple and solemn and as soon as it was over the guest
poured out for the beginning of the fun, while the man and wife
withdrew to sign the register.

Persons of all ages now thronged the roadway below the church
Women and girls had clambered onto half a dozen jaunting cars
and men and boys had mounted, two and even three together, to
the bare backs of horses.

Other guests, perhaps not so close to the happy union, were
prepared to walk the three-mile stretch to the new home. But
there was no hurry about starting.

A fiddler arrived and the dance was on. One after another the
young men volunteered, or responded to calls, and showed their
prowess on the hard earth of the road, while the crowd kept time
and cheered. We found the 24-hour jubilee in full blast. A
concertina had been added to the orchestra and a second and a
third fiddler appeared later. Into a kitchen of not more than
twelve by fourteen feet fully sixty persons had crowded in the
form of a hollow square, with space in the middle for four
dancers. Here old and young couples were succeeding each other
in jigs and reels, and the old seemed equally accomplished and
more persistent. The light was dim because the door was low and
the two windows small. The August day was warm for the Arans,
and a mingled odor of turf smoke and moist woolens pervaded the
room.

In the adjacent bedchamber, toward which I wedged my way
behind the hospitable bridegroom, tea was being served, together
with broken loaves and cake.'

DEATH

Death to the islander is an accepted part of the condition of living. As in rural Ireland generally, a corpse is 'waked' in the house until it is taken to the church on the afternoon of the day following the death.

Friends and neighbours gather to pay their respects to the dead person and to condole with the family. On entering the house a caller kneels by the bed where the corpse is laid out and prays briefly. Sympathy is offered to members of the immediate family and the caller joins the other mourners in the kitchen.

The reponse to an individual's death is related to the circumstances. If the death was sudden and tragic, as in the case of a young man drowned at sea or a mother with young children dying at childbirth, the mourners spend the night consoling and supporting the relatives. If, on the other hand, the deceased has been old, or ailing for a long time, the wake is looked on as a meeting of friends. The dead person will be praised, his merits recalled and stories related concerning his skill as farmer or fisherman. Drink will be distributed to the mourners and the atmosphere of the wake house will reflect an optimistic acceptance of the fact of death rather than a sense of irretrievable loss.

In some cases a *Caoine* may be sung — a mourning verse which consists of expressions of loss and sorrow repeated at length in a subdued voice which rises to a loud moan occasionally. Certain old women are regarded as expert 'keeners' and may be found keeping vigil beside the corpse at all wakes in their neighbourhood.

The attendance at a wake reflects the esteem and affection in which a deceased person was held by the community. The family are deeply honoured by a good turn out and will reciprocate the gesture to each of the mourners when the occasion arises.

Tomás Ó Crohan writes about the tragic death of his eldest son. He exemplifies the islanders' acceptance of tragedy and mourning as part of their lot.

'At the time when the young birds come and are beginning to mature, the lads used to go after them. My eldest boy and the King's son planned to go to a place where they were likely to get a young gull — for one of those would often live among the chickens in a house for a year and more.

The two went together after the nests to bring a pair or so of the birds home with them. They were in a bad place, and, as my

boy was laying hold of the young gull, it flew up and he fell dow
the cliff, out on the sea, God save the hearers! He remained afloa
on the surface for a long time until a canoe going after lobste
came up and took him aboard.

His grandfather (his mother's father) was in the canoe tha
took him in. We had only one comfort — there was no wound o
blemish anywhere on his body, though it was a steep fall fror
the cliff. We must endure it and be content! It was a great solac
to me that he could be brought ashore and not left to the merc
of the sea. This was the first beginning, and an ill one it was, Go
help us!

This happened about the year 1890, just when the boy wa
developing and beginning to lend a hand. Well, those that pas
cannot feed those that remain, and we, too, had to put out ou
oars again and drive on.'

SPECIAL FESTIVALS

In the Aran islands, the Christian festivals of Easter an
Christmas are observed with great celebration as are the holy day
of important local and national saints. The islanders also celebrat
special festivals which are closely associated with the fertility o
the land and which probably originated in pre-Christian times
These festivals are celebrated by rural communities, not alone ir
Ireland, but all over Europe, wherever the cycle of crop growtl
dominates the pattern of work.

The festivals have Christian names but the rituals are almost th
same as in the Celtic era.

ST. BRIGID'S DAY (February 1st)

St. Brigid's Day signals the beginning of the year's work on the
farm. Crosses made of straw, which in Celtic times symbolised the
sun but are now called St. Brigid's crosses, are placed on the inne
side of the thatched roof to protect the family during the coming
year. The accumulation of crosses over the years indicates the age
of many old houses. Young boys may visit neighbouring houses
carrying a straw effigy (meant to represent St. Brigid) and be
rewarded with a small gift. A loaf of bread, or a potato, is sometimes placed on the doorstep to keep hunger away from the house
during the year.

Men and women at Kilronan, 1890. The men wear the home-spun woollen trousers and waistcoat, with knitted 'ganseys' and caps. The women wear the petticoats and multi-coloured shawls of the islands.

MAY DAY (May 1st)

May 1st is the first day of summer. A green branch is brought into the house and kept there throughout the season. The song *Thugamar féin an Samradh Linn* ("We have brought the summer with us") is associated with this custom. Great care is taken on May Eve and May Day to ensure that cattle, butter and water will be unharmed by malevolent fairies or spirits. Some people consider that weather and cloud patterns on May Day are an indication of how the harvest will fare.

ST. JOHN'S EVE (June 23rd)

The Christian churches celebrate the feast of St. John but this date also corresponds with the ancient festival of Midsummer. Bonfires blaze in many villages throughout Ireland and lighted branches from these fires may be thrown into the fields where crops are growing in order to bring good luck. Cattle are driven between two bonfires to ensure that their calves will be healthy.

SAMHAIN (November 1st)

Hallowe'en, the eve of All Saint's Day, corresponds with an ancient feast to commemorate the dead. The spirits of the dead are believed to wander abroad on this night. People remain at home, special games are played and bread is thrown against the door to banish hunger during the coming winter.

the family

HE FAMILY IS THE MOST IMPORTANT social unit on the islands. Together, the members of the immediate or nuclear family form a labour force to carry out the regular duties in the home and on the farm. Large families are regarded as a blessing in Aran and households with ten, twelve, or even more children are not uncommon. But all of these children will not live to reach adulthood. Infant mortality, distance from medical aid and the hazards of the fisherman's work, will ensure that some of them will precede their parents to the grave.

Childlessness is regarded as a misfortune to which there are few parallels. Therefore, when a marriage has taken place conception and childbirth are anxiously awaited by both the young couple and their parents. The successful birth of a healthy child is an occasion of great joy as it means a continuation of the family name on the land.

Children are named with care and pride. Local national saints names, such as Enda, Coile (Coley), Gobnait and Patrick are popular and will be found repeated in each succeeding generation of a particular family. Because so many children are named for their grandparents, or for an aunt or uncle, confusion is inevitable and many of the islanders share the same christian names and surnames. The individuals in such cases are distinguished by nicknames derived from the christian names of their fathers and grandfathers. For example, Tomás Ó Flatharta, the son of Paid Ó Flatharta may be known as Tomás Phaidi to distinguish him from others of the same name. In cases where a woman inherits land and her husband is landless the children will receive a maternal nickname. Seán Ó Sé, the son of Maire and Paidi will in such a case be known as Seán Mhaire.

The 1901 census records show that a total of 61 different surnames were represented on the islands but certain names such as Flaherty, Conneely and Dirrane occurred much more frequently than others.

HEAD OF THE FAMILY

The father is usually the dominant member of the family and is regarded by outsiders as representing the whole family. The farm is known by his name and the farm house and most of the goods descend from father to son along with the patronym. Decisions with regard to farming and fishing are made by the father, though frequently there is informal consultation with the other members of the family.

The mother's sphere of influence is confined to the work of the house and farmyard. The tasks which recur daily are regarded as the province of the woman. These include cooking, washing, cleaning, churning, bread-making, spinning and clothes-making, within the home; and the feeding and care of chickens and other fowl, and perhaps the pigs, within the farmyard. Generally the older boys help the father in his tasks; girls and younger boys are the assistants of the mother and are subject to her discipline.

Even though the father is regarded as the formal head the mother may exert a considerable influence on the family through her management of the home and through her direction of the children. In some instances a woman may be the dominant partner in the family's dealings with the community. This is frowned on by the islanders and an ideal relationship is considered to exist between a couple who are equally competent in their individual tasks and who defer to each other by consultation and display of mutual respect.

THE WOMAN'S ROLE

After marriage the Aran woman tends to merge her identity with that of her husband and her new family. Her interest will focus on the home and she may come to regard outside events as having little bearing on her life. The Aran woman's expectations are largely bound up with the rearing of her family and she derives her main satisfaction from the progress of its members through life. The bonds between parents and children are of an enduring kind and loyalty to family is a quality on which community opinion places great emphasis.

KINSHIP

Many households are comprised of three generations. Paternal grandfathers and grandmothers of the children live in the house and are an integral part of the organisation of daily life. Family structure is not confined to the immediate family group but extends a network of relationships outwards to a larger kin grouping. Every islander belongs to such an extended family grouping, which he or she will refer to as *mo mhuintear.* Great pleasure is taken in reciting lists of cousins and marriage relations and even quite young people display a fascination with their family linkages, showing a consciousness of belonging to this larger group. The kin group provides a support system for the individual and his family. He can confidently call on his kinfold in times of crisis or distress but, even more importantly, he shares his everyday work and leisure with them. They will assist him in the saving of the harvest, the building of a house or the thatching of a roof; they may form part of his curragh crew, or join with him to purchase nets. This system of mutual help and obligation is invaluable, particularly in an area where money is scarce and may be insufficient to hire labour.

This exchanging of labour or 'cooring' will also involve the immediate relatives of a man's spouse, who become members of his and his children's kin groups.

CHANGE IN THE FAMILY

Marriage is a crucial event in Aran family life. The old farmer and his wife give up their title to house and land and retire from active management. The young man and his bride assume control and from then on the farm is regarded as theirs.

Though the old couple remain on in the home it is regarded as desirable that all others should leave in order to present a fair opportunity to the young couple who are starting a new family. Unmarried sons may emigrate, or in some cases, marry and build a house of their own, though without farm property they know that there is little opportunity for them to survive in their own

Father and son, Kilronan 1890. The growing boy begins to spend more and more time in his father's company learning from him the skills of farming, and later, of fishing.

ommunity. Unmarried daughters may themselves marry and move to their new husband's home, but the isolated and numerically limited community offers few partners of suitable ge, many of whom are in any case too closely related to satisfy he requirements of Church and State. The old parents and the brother who has assumed ownership will seek to create a good natch for each daughter but many women follow the footsteps f their bachelor brothers to England and America.

A smooth transition of ownership and control is vital to the happiness and well-being of all concerned: the old order changes nd a new generation in the family tree is created. Not least, the in group, on which the family can rely for mutual aid, is xtended and consolidated through the links with the 'new' wife's amily.

THE KIN GROUP AND EMIGRATION

It is not just in relation to farming and fishing on the island that the kin group functions. Members of the extended family will maintain the bonds and sense of obligation even when separated by three thousand miles of ocean. Thus children who have emigrated will regularly send gifts of money to their parents in order to assist them in rearing the younger members of the family. Even an aunt or uncle may perform this service particularly at Christmas time. This inflow of cash is a vital component in the precarious economic balance on which island life depends.

The kin group also forms a channel through which emigration can take place, making the journey to a strange land less hazardous and intimidating. In fact this link has facilitated emigration from the islands since the Famine. An emigrant, whether male or female, plays an important role in making possible the migration of brothers and sisters and even nephews and nieces. Money is sent home for the fare and expenses, a job is sought on behalf of the new immigrant who is cushioned during the first difficult years of exile by a group of relatives and friends.

His native language is of no economic value in his new situation serving only to isolate him from the mainstream of American life but it helps him and his fellows to preserve their bonds of loyalty and affection in an alien environment and he may continue to use it among friends and relatives from Aran for years after he first emigrates.

Emigration to America in most cases means taking up a permanent home and livelihood in a new country. Both he and his parents know that they will probably never meet again. The finality of separation has something of the anguish associated with death. It is hardly surprising then to find the sending-off gathering for a young emigrant described as an "American Wake". Music singing and dancing will take place but a more sombre note almost one of mourning, underlies the gaiety and is never far from the surface of the apparently cheerful gathering.

An emigrant may spend forty or fifty years in the country of his adoption and may die without seeing his native land again but contact with home will usually be maintained, if only by way of the annual card at Christmas.

ϽΟΟΘRΠ
ΘRΘΠ

SOME FEATURES OF LIFE on the Aran Islands have undergone little change in the past fifty years but in many respects the way of life made famous by Synge has disappeared forever. The population has continued to decline throughout the twentieth century and emigration has drained the life-blood from the community. Tourism and the mass media have brought the outside world into every Aran home. The most important change of all has been the growth of the islanders' desire to develop their economic resources in order to achieve the standard of living which is taken for granted elsewhere in Ireland.

FARMING

Farming is still important in the island economy but the people are no longer as dependent on it for their livelihood as they were in the past. The spade and the scythe have not been replaced by modern machinery as the Aran farms are too small to allow for the purchase of machinery and the fields too tiny and rocky to allow its use.

The population has declined steadily since the mid-nineteenth century affecting the size and ownership of farms. Frequently, all but one of the children in a particular family emigrated leaving one son at home to manage the land and care for their parents. Should this remaining son not marry, as was often the case, the land passed, on his death, to a nephew or cousin, and was amalgamated with this relative's holding. Thus, the number of farms on the Aran Islands dropped from a total of 373 in 1927 to

349 in 1960. The land which made up the 'vanished' farms wa added to other farms and helped to increase the number c holdings containing 20 hectares or more and to bring three farm over the 40 hectares mark. There has been no change in the tot number of holdings during the last 17 years.

The Irish Government set up an Interdepartmental Committee in 1957, to examine the problems facing small farms on th Western Seaboard. This committee concluded that there could b no hope of improving the standard of living of small farmer without bringing about a huge increase in average farm size. The felt that farmers could not possibly make an acceptable living o farms of 12 hectares or less.

The majority of holdings on the Aran Islands are small. Thirt of them are merely one acre potato patches and an additiona 173 holdings have less than 12 hectares each. All of these holding contain tracts of infertile land and bare rock as well as thei potato gardens and strips of grazing. Average farm income is ver low and most of these farms, could not, even in the most favour able circumstances, yield an adequate family income.

Irish membership of the European Economic Community ha made the plight of the small farmer even worse. The Communit: has plans for developing agriculture in the member countrie which involves the phasing out of smaller farms. Under it Mansholdt Plan proposals the majority of Aran farms would b regarded as too small to be developed to a level where they coul provide an income comparable to that provided by industrial jobs In the eyes of the EEC such farms are not qualified to receiv grants and loans to increase productivity.

The last fifty years have seen the development of a number o large farms on Aran. The owners of these farms may be able tc make a living solely from their land but the future for the average Aran farmer is bleak unless work is created for him in industry tourism or fishing.

Changes in farm size and in family life style have brought abou a number of adjustments in the type of farming activities in which the islanders engage. There has been a general decline in the number of acres of crops planted each year since the beginning of the century. In 1925 a total of 221 hectares of crops were plantec but by 1973 this figure had fallen to less than 53 hectares.

The potato is still the most important crop but the number o acres planted has decreased each year. In 1925 a total of 40 hectares of potatoes were grown but this figure had dropped tc

New house types have changed the Island landscape. The traditional thatched roof has proved too costly to repair and replace and the skills of masonry have been generally replaced by the use of concrete blocks. The pony and trap is an ideal vehicle in which to tour the islands.

80 hectares by 1960 as the declining population needed to produce less food. Since 1960, however, the potato acreage has rapidly decreased reaching an all time low of 38 hectares in 1973 completely outpacing the continuing population decline. The potato, then, seems to have lost some of its importance as the diet of the islanders became more varied and relied less on the traditional staples. A limited amount of cabbage, turnips and other vegetables are also sown for domestic use.

Corn crops have suffered a similar decline. A total of 58 hectares of rye and just over 1 hectare of oats and barley were planted in 1925. By 1960 the total acreage had dropped to 2. reflecting the decline in the use of rye as a roofing material. Imported roof tiles have proved cheaper to erect and maintain on new houses and many of the older thatched-roof houses have fallen into disrepair as occupants emigrated or died. The manual labour involved in planting, reaping, flailing and winnowing rye without the aid of machinery, has been another deterrent and may lead, eventually, to the disappearance of the thatched roof from the island landscape. In 1973 only 5 hectares of rye and 5 hectares of oats were planted.

CATTLE

Farmers have moved away from tillage and increasingly devoted their land to cattle rearing. The islander no longer seeks to provide for all the needs of his family but concentrates, rather, on those activities which are most profitable. Cattle prices have risen considerably in the past decade and they received an added boost with Irish entry into the EEC in 1973. The hardy island cattle are popular with buyers as they are easily fattened when grazed on fertile grassland for a few months. Cattle rearing makes for an easier work load and is therefore popular with the many elderly farmers and the younger farmer-fishermen.

Between 1960 and 1973 cattle numbers, on the islands, rose by 40% though there were yearly fluctuations depending on market demand and price. The jobbers come to the monthly fairs on all three islands to bargain for the cattle which, when sold, the farmer undertakes to ship to Galway at his own expense.

Almost all families still keep one or two dairy cows to supply their domestic requirements. Islanders who have no cows buy milk from their neighbours. Bottled milk is sometimes imported during the summer months to satisfy the demand created by the ιflux of tourists.

A few families still churn milk to make butter for their own se but the practice is in decline and most people buy butter ιnported from mainland creameries. In 1974 a total of 517 kg. f home-butter was made.

Sheep numbers have declined rapidly in recent years as farmers witched to cattle production. The 1960 total of 2879 sheep had ιllen to 465 by 1973 and most of the wool for knitting was ιnported from the mainland.

Pigs are no longer reared on Aran and the number of poultry ιas halved in the past 15 years. These and other changes emphasise ιe passing of self-sufficiency, the concentration on more ommercial aspects of farming and the changes in the family ιet.

FISHING

The fishing industry in the Aran Islands, as in the rest of ιreland, has had varying fortunes in the years since 1900. The ιrst World War brought a temporary boom to the mackerel fishery ιut was immediately followed by a period of stagnation and ιecline. Markets were limited, processing facilities and ice plants ιere non-existent and the boats and equipment of the Irish fleet ιould not match those of their foreign competitors. The Irish Sea ιisheries Association was set up by the Government in 1931 to ιelp modernise the industry but the lack of a home market for ιsh retarded any significant development.

In the last decade, however, the fishing industry has boomed ιn Aran and the island fleet, based at Kilronan, is one of the finest ιn the country, employing a total of 85 full time fishermen. This ιvelcome development is a direct result of the work undertaken ιy the Fisheries Association's successor, Bord Iascaigh Mhara – ιhe Sea Fisheries Board. B.I.M., as it is known, trains fishermen ιnd skippers, helps them to acquire boats, provides port facilities, ιaises the quality of fish in the market-place through icing and ιroper handling and promotes the eating of fish among the general ιublic.

The Aran Fleet consists of 21 wooden-hulled boats of 9 metres ιeel length and upwards. It is based at Kilronan as there is no ιther pier of suitable size in any of the islands. Six of these boats ιre large trawlers, nine are medium-sized trawlers and the others ιre half-decked lobster boats. The boats are owned and crewed by full time fishermen from all three islands. Seventeen Aran men have been trained as skippers on B.I.M. and Fisheries Department courses and are qualified to operate the modern trawlers which Irish boatyards are now producing. A large trawler at present cost from £250,000 to £1,000,000 depending on size and equipment The purchaser must pay 5% deposit and he receives a grant of 25% of the total cost from B.I.M. and F.E.O.G.A., the EEC development agency. The balance of the cost can be borrowed through B.I.M. at a special interest rate and repaid in regular instalments

During the 19th century, trawlers depended on sails to propel them but the modern trawler is equipped with a powerful diesel engine. Other equipment includes a winch to pull in the net and a power-block to help lift large catches aboard.

A trawl is a bag-shaped net which is towed over smooth patches of sea bed. The mouth of the net is kept open, vertically, by weighting the ground line and attaching floats to the headline otter boards (or 'trawl doors') drag the sides of the net outwards. This type of net catches cod, haddock, sole, plaice and other fish which feed on, or near the sea-bed.

A trawl net can also be used to kill shoals of mackerel and herring which swim nearer the surface. Two trawlers, working as a pair, tow the net and thus manage to keep it open without letting it sink to the sea-bed. The larger Aran boats all participate in the herring fishery, travelling to ports all round Ireland in search of shoals. A valuable winter and spring herring fishery has developed in Galway Bay so for part of the year, at least, good catches can be made without having to venture too far from the home port. The herring are lightly salted, or smoked, and exported to the Continent.

The modern trawler is equipped with a range of electronic aids for communication, navigation and fish-finding. It contains comfortable accommodation and cooking facilities for the crew as the boat may often be at sea overnight. The more recently built boats have centrally heated cabins and a shower room Trawler men work long and irregular hours and are paid a share of the money realised by the catch rather than a fixed wage When everything goes well the rewards are good but when fish are scarce, or the weather exceptionally bad, the fisherman may have a very meagre return for his work.

In addition to the trawler fleet, twenty-eight smaller boats many of them curraghs, work from beaches and small piers in all three islands. They are powered by oars and outboard engines

An 11 metre lobster boat, part of the modern fleet which has transformed the economy of the islands by providing employment for young men who would otherwise have to emigrate. However inflation on the price of new boats has put even relatively small lobster boats beyond the reach of Aran fishermen, who must bear heavier fuel costs and transport costs than the mainland fishermen.

and each is crewed by two or three part-time fishermen who fish with lobster pots and hand lines in summer.

Lobster fishing is carried on in the traditional manner but the modern, wooden-hulled and motor powered boats can handle many more pots and range further from port than the curraghs ever could. Their work is made easier and safer by electronic aids such as the echo-sounder and the radio telephone. The curragh, however, does retain an advantage in that it can be used from Inishmaan and Inisheer where the larger boats would find it difficult to land.

Lobster fishing is a seasonal activity which is dependent on fine weather and calm seas for its success. Lobster and crayfish are delicacies and fetch high prices on the French and Spanish markets but the huge crab catch must be dumped as there is no plant which could process and market them.

The salmon is one of the most valuable fish resources in Aran waters. Each year, in early summer, the mature salmon swim from their feeding grounds in the North Atlantic to their spawning grounds in Irish rivers. But the islanders are prohibited from fishing for salmon, only a few being licensed to catch them with drift nets. A proportion of the salmon must reach the spawning grounds if the species is to survive and, in addition, riverside angling is an important tourist attraction. It is obvious then, that conservation measures are necessary.

Private individuals and companies, though, have legal rights to kill numbers of the fish at the mouths of the rivers. The islanders feel aggrieved that commercial and tourism interests should be catered for while they, isolated as they are from other means of earning a living, are debarred from one of their few potential sources of income. Salmon swim past their island to fuel the mainland economy while emigration continues from Aran and while its inhabitants have to tolerate a standard of living which is lower than that found elsewhere in Ireland.

The rapid development of the fishing industry in the past decade has brought a new prosperity to the Aran islands, particularly to Inishmore, and has done much to halt population decline as young men take to the fishing boat rather than to the emigrant ship. Kilronan pier has recently been improved and the Government has plans to develop Rossaveal, on the Galway mainland, as a convenient landing place for Aran fishermen, as it is only one hour's journey from Inishmore. At present an Aran boat must make a five hour round trip to the Galway docks to land its catch or to refuel. This journey will be eliminated when the new pier at Rossaveal is completed and the harbour dredged to accommodate the larger boats. It is hoped to provide an ice-making plant and a fresh water supply at Rossaveal, where there are already facilities for storing lobsters and processing herring.

But there are major problems which must be solved if the industry is to enjoy further development. The deposit required to buy a new trawler is beyond the means of many young fisher-men. Grant and loan facilities are, at present, not available for the purchase of cheap second-hand vessels, even though such boats offer the best opportunity to young men wishing to start out on their own. There are nine qualified skippers working as deckhands in the Aran fleet who could form the basis for the next phase of expansion in the industry.

Fish prices in Ireland are still well below those obtained by the fishermen of other European countries but fuel and gear costs have risen rapidly putting the Irish fisherman at a disadvantage even though he is near to some of the richest fishing grounds in Europe.

But the greatest threat to future prosperity lies in the over-fishing of stocks, particularly by huge fleets of foreign trawlers. The fishermen say that Ireland needs a properly policed "50 mile limit" to its territorial waters within which the boats of other nations would not be allowed to fish. They argue that it is only in such a situation that we can properly conserve stocks and plan the further expansion of the fishing industry.

TOURISM

Tourism is now an important source of income for the Aran Islands. Visitors, from elsewhere in Ireland as well as from other countries, come to the islands in ever-increasing numbers. Some come to learn Irish or improve their command of the language, others to study the unusual geology and flora, or the remarkable collection of ancient remains found on the islands. But the major-ity come to sample a special way of life, made famous throughout the world by island writers, as well as by a continuous stream of outside writers and artists who have followed in Synge's footsteps to these bare Atlantic rocks where can be found *ciúneas gan uaigneas* — solitude without loneliness.

In recent years an improved schedule of sailings from Galway, and the introduction of regular Aer Arann flights, has increased the number of holidaymakers and day-trippers, particularly in the summer months.

A restaurant has been established at Kilronan and a small hotel has functioned there for some time and many of the families have built extensions on to their houses to accommodate guests. This practice is gradually changing the traditional nature of the islands' homes and family life.

The tourist trade is hindered in its expansion by a number of factors. It can only offer part-time employment and there is frequently an acute shortage of help in the guest houses during the summer high-season. The uncertainty of the piped water supply poses problems for catering, hygiene and sanitation during dry spells. The ever increasing swarms of day-trippers are of little financial benefit to the tourist industry which has not as yet, begun to service this market.

The tourist inspires mixed feelings in the islander. His arrival brings an inflow of money, a rise in employment, albeit seasonal, and an important boost to the self-esteem of the community through the interest shown in, and the value placed on, their way of life.

But the tourist also brings an image of his own way of life with him, an image which is frequently one of material prosperity and urban glamour beside which island life may appear harsh and unpromising to restless young people. Some of the older islanders regret the advent of the tourist, regarding him as one of the reasons for the decline in traditional customs and the language in the Kilronan area, and the continuing migration of young people. Inishmaan and Inisheer have felt less of the impact, in both its positive and negative aspects of tourism. Due to their isolation and difficulties of access they are more liable to attract the language enthusiast than the day tripper.

Inisheer, in particular, benefits from a summer college for students of the Irish language, which attracts large groups of young people from all parts of Ireland to its month-long courses.

OTHER INDUSTRIES

In 1975, a factory was built on Inishmore. It was run by a jewellery company from Birmingham, who employed twelve girls, having sent them to England for training. But this company did not stay long on Aran: and in the summer of 1976 they closed the factory. However, it was soon re-opened by a Dublin based

Modern Aran. Cured sheepskins and traditional Aran knitwear for sale to tourists. Tourism is assuming a major importance in the Aran economy but regretfully, many of the handcrafts sold on the islands are imported and a valuable potential source of employment is ignored.

electronics firm, subsidised by Gaeltarra Eireann. (Gaeltarra Eireann is a State-funded body which seeks to create employment in Gaeltacht areas). A group of young people, some of whom were previously employed in the jewellery plant, are being re-trained for this new kind of work. It is hoped that this firm will ultimately employ about 40 people.

Only factories which manufacture small objects made from raw materials which are neither bulky nor perishable could hope to be successful on Aran, as freight costs would otherwise be crippling. The islanders are hopeful that this new venture will survive the many obstacles associated with isolation and distance from markets.

There are some craft shops but these do not only sell goods made on the islands. Some women knit sweaters or weave crioses and sell them to tourists, but this is time-consuming and expensive, as the wool has to be bought and imported from the mainland.

Kelp is no longer burned in Aran, but there are still markets for Aran seaweed. The acid obtained by processing seaweed is used in the preparation of a wide variety of products such as cosmetics and medicines, and the stems of the red seaweed, so plentiful in Aran, are particularly rich in it.

Nowadays the collected weed is shipped to the mainland for processing. Great piles of gathered weed awaiting shipping are a common sight on the piers. However, freight charges are very high and eat into profits made by the sale of seaweed.

HOUSES

The long, low, thatched cottage, so long a feature of the Aran landscape, is no longer the dominant house type. Some of the traditional cottages have been adapted to changing times by the addition of extra rooms and tiled roofs. Many bungalows have been built, similar in design to those found in town and country elsewhere in Ireland. The Department of the Gaeltacht for a time promoted the building of two storey houses, but these are generally agreed to be less suited, than single storey houses, to the climatic conditions found on the islands.

FUEL AND POWER

The Aran Islands have never been connected to the Irish

Inishmaan and Inisheer do not as yet have piers where the Naomh Eanna can land to discharge cargo. A wide range of imported goods are ferried ashore in curraghs. Bottled gas is widely used for cooking and lighting and coal has almost completely replaced turf as a fuel.

POPULATION FIGURES FOR ARAN

Year	Inisheer	Inishmaan	Inishmore	Total
1901	483	421	1,959	2,863
1911	480	420	1,779	2,679
1926	409	380	1,368	2,157
1936	445	375	1,289	2,109
1946	447	388	1,136	1,971
1951	388	361	1,019	1,768
1956	376	361	944	1,681
1961	358	357	933	1,648
1966	345	342	925	1,612
1971	313	319	864	1,496

National Electricity Grid and, until recently, the inhabitants have had to forego the convenience and comfort which the electricity user enjoys. The lack of a cheap, efficient power supply also discouraged industries which might otherwise have come to the islands.

A successful campaign for this basic service resulted in a diesel-engined electricity generator being installed on Inisheer. A similar system began to produce power for Inishmore in December 1975. The Department of the Gaeltacht has now provided a grant of £100,000 to pay for a scheme on Inishmaan, to be completed by summer 1977.

Electricity is expensive, costing about twice as much, per unit consumed, on the islands as it does on the mainland. Co-operatives have had to be set up by the island people to service the generators and maintain supplies, at their own expense, as the national Electricity Supply Board is only responsible for the mainland network. The cost of maintenance is high because materials and skilled labour must be imported. In order to solve this problem the Inishmaan Co-operative has recruited an apprentice diesel fitter who is now undergoing training with AnCO, the Industrial Training Authority.

Turf, coal and paraffin oil are still used as fuel for fires and heating but the cost of these commodities has risen steeply in recent years. Heavy freight charges add further to the cost of turf and coal. The Inishmaan Co-op is now supplying almost all of that island's coal in order to reduce the cost through bulk buying.

WATER SUPPLY

The supply of fresh water, both for domestic use and for farm animals, has always posed a problem in the Aran Islands. Rainfall is adequate but the exposed limestone pavements are permeable and make a very poor water catchment surface. Inishmore now has a water scheme serving all parts of the island. Motor-driven pumps distribute water from the main reservoir, situated on the clifftop near Dún Aengus, to the houses. On the other islands small reservoirs serve groups of houses but many people still must depend on spring wells and rain troughs for their supply. Despite these improvements, water is still scarce on Aran. The islands were badly affected by the recent summer droughts. Water levels in reservoirs were so low that the water supply had to be cut off for a certain number of hours each day.

Water supply remains a problem in the arid limestone landscape. Inishmore now has a water scheme but wells like this are still the only source of supply for many homes on all three islands.

Some time ago, one of the spring-wells on Inishmore was polluted: to fetch water, a man used the drum in which he carried diesel-oil for his tractor. It took a long time before the water in the well was drinkable again. It was the islanders' first experience of water pollution. Now a sign painted on the rock near the well asks its users to keep it clean.

TRANSPORT AND COMMUNICATION

Maintaining contact with the mainland has remained a problem for the islanders. The *Dun Aengus* a sturdy little Dublin-built steamer, initially owned by the Galway Bay Steamship Company, and later by Coras Iompair Eireann (C.I.E.) sailed between Galway and the islands, carrying passengers and cargoes for almost 50 years. In 1958, when she was taken off the route and broken up, she was the oldest steamer in regular service in Western Europe.

She was replaced by the MV *Naomh Eanna*, also Dublin-built, a larger and more efficient steamer. The *Naomh Eanna* runs several times a week all the year round (except during her short annual overhaul).

Passengers being ferried ashore to Inishmaan from the Naomh Eanna. The influx of tourists in the summer months represents a valuable boost to the economy. The introduction of the Aer Arann service of daily flights has been of benefit to islander and tourist alike.

Another vessel, the MV *Galway Bay* sails daily from Galway to Kilronan during the summer, and in the winter when the *Naomh Eanna* is being overhauled. It is also owned by C.I.E.

A privately owned cruiser the *Queen of Aran* sails regularly from Rossaveal on the Connemara coast. This is a short run — it only takes about one hour to sail from Rossaveal to Kilronan. Regular motorboat sailings from Doolin, Co. Clare, to Inisheer are held daily in the summer, and, if the weather is suitable, by request in the winter.

The islanders would like to see a daily scheduled service established and they have approached Government agencies with a view to the setting up of a roll-on roll-off car ferry service. They also feel that the Government should subsidise the transport of goods to the islands as most goods cost 20% — 30% more than they do on the mainland due to high transport costs. It is generally conceded that building materials, being heavy and bulky, are up to 100% more expensive for the prospective housebuilder on the islands of Inishmaan and Inisheer, where there are no suitable piers to accommodate the steamer.

AER ARANN

In 1970 Aer Arann began operating a regular air service between the Aran Islands and Galway. This has done a great deal to improve the islands' contact with the mainland.

Until 1970, all emergencies had been dealt with by the Life Boat Service – patients who had to be taken to mainland hospitals, as well as boats in trouble at sea. The islanders became more and more aware that the service was inadequate. Firstly, the vessel in use was equipped with few navigational aids which meant that any voyage in rough seas or at night was dangerous and lengthy. Secondly, the lifeboat rides at anchor in Kilronan bay and in high seas is very difficult to reach by curragh or rowing boat. Thirdly, money was scarce as the Lifeboat Service was financed completely by voluntary subscriptions. Finally it was a most unsuitable way of bringing emergency medical cases to the mainland – people in need of immediate hospitalisation or surgery and women about to give birth faced a long, cold uncomfortable journey which often caused further complications.

The islanders were determined that this should change, and made their plight known to the national newspapers. One article, which listed the advantages of setting up an island air-service was read by a group of Galway business men, who decided that they would back the plan financially. So, in 1970, Aer Arann, an independent company subsidised by Gaeltarra Eireann was set up.

At first the service just operated between Galway and Killeany in Inishmore. However, since 1973, Inishmaan has also been included in the daily flight schedule. When Inisheer's runway is completed, it will be a three-island service.

The island runways are levelled sand dunes, sown ·vith grass which form a hard dry surface. They have no facilities such as re-fuelling points: the planes are refuelled in Galway.

Aer Arann now has four ten seater (9 passengers and pilot) Britten-Norman "Islander" aircraft on the route. These planes are specially designed for short journeys between islands, and for short take-off and landings. The company employs four pilots and a small staff.

There are daily flights all year round, the frequency on any given day varying with the number of passengers or the amount of freight to be carried.

Aer Arann, more than any other single innovation, has changed the quality of life on the islands as it has bestowed a new freedom of movement on the inhabitants and established much closer contact with the mainland. The islanders feel that Aer Arann deserves a Government subsidy in the form of tax free fuel, similar to the concession already enjoyed by Aer Lingus and C.I.E.

TRANSPORT ON THE ISLANDS

For most people small donkey or horse carts are still the main form of transport on Aran but the number of cars has been increasing on Inishmore, since the first one arrived in 1959. Distances are too short on the other islands for a car to be of any use.

Tractors are used on all three islands; a few each on Inishmaan and Inisheer and a larger number on Inishmore. They are not used, however, for farmwork because the land is too rocky and the fields too small for this to be possible. Instead they are utilised to haul merchandise in from the ferry, or to collect coal and turf from the piers.

Motorbikes are common. The islanders find them useful and economical to run over the short distances. The bicycle is, of course, very useful and popular for travel on the islands. The possession of mechanically propelled vehicles presents problems which do not exist on the mainland. There are no filling stations on the islands, so all petrol and diesel fuel has to be imported in drums. This presents a further difficulty, since, for insurance reasons, the ferry boat will not carry fuel in its hold. The islanders have to find other ways of importing their petrol. Furthermore, cars have to be taken to the mainland or parts have to be brought out to the islands for servicing and maintenance, both operations involving heavy freight charges.

Except for the few tarred "main" roads on Inishmore, roads on Aran are dirt tracks. The car owners complain that the bumpy dirt roads ruin their cars, and the horse and donkey owners complain that the tarred-roads do not give their animals enough grip!

COMMUNICATIONS

Mail arrives from the mainland twice a week and is distributed from the various post-offices — one in Kilronan and one in Kilmurvey on Inishmore, and one each in Inishmaan and Inisheer.

The islands were linked telegraphically to the mainland by submarine cable at the beginning of this century. In the early 1920's the Kilronan telephone exchange was installed but it was not until 1960 and 1961, respectively that Inishmaan and Inisheer got theirs. Private telephones, however, are only common on Inishmore, where there are 10 lines and 72 telephones.

For a long time, the people on Aran have had battery-operated radios, and the establishment of Radio na Gaeltachta (an Irish language radio service) in 1972 has made available a greater number of broadcasts in the Irish language. Many homes now also have television sets.

EDUCATION

All three islands have had their own primary schools since the end of the nineteenth century but until recently those wishing to avail of secondary education have had to attend boarding schools on the mainland with the aid of a special scholarship scheme for Gaeltacht children. Such an education, however, prepared the children for a range of job opportunities which were available only in mainland towns and cities.

A Vocational school was established at Kilronan in 1954 providing courses which are more likely to equip a young person to occupy a place within the local economy. The school is co-educational and at present there are seven full-time teachers and seventy students. Students from Inishmaan and Inisheer lodge with families on Inishmore and return home only at weekends. The school has now developed to include a senior section and students wishing to pursue a Leaving Certificate course no longer have to attend a mainland boarding school.

A full range of subjects are taught, with the exception of metal-work, for which there are no facilities at present. The principal teacher would also like to introduce a building construction course, in the near future. As there are only two builders on the islands there is a need for such a course and it would undoubtedly prove popular with adults as well as with the regular students.

JOB PROSPECTS

Job prospects have improved for boys with the development of the fishing industry. Young people, who have left the islands during the last decade, are now returning to work on local trawlers. The Inishmore factory can only employ a limited number and the guesthouses provide work which is, of its nature, seasonal and temporary. Many girls must still leave in search of employment and most will eventually marry in the mainland and settle permanently there.

LEISURE

The young have a range of leisure pursuits available to them on Inishmore. Céilís and film shows are held in the parish hall on a weekly basis throughout the year and more frequently in summer. The youth club, based in the school, and the public house pool table cater for various groups and a local committee arranges football matches and other sporting events. Almost all of the homes have a radio and many are acquiring television sets now that electricity is available. However, the traditional housewalking continues to some extent, even today.

The Pattern or Patrún, is the great social event of the year. In the past it was customary to visit the holy places on the islands or to travel to the mainland to pray at shrines and holy wells on Pattern day. Nowadays the focus is on sporting competitions. Curragh races are held and are the subject of intense rivalry between crews from each 'village'. Tug-o-war competitions, bicycle races, children's sports and dancing are popular on all three islands.

THE LANGUAGE

Irish remains the everyday language of the Aran Islands despite the ever-increasing contact with the English-speaking mainland through tourism and the mass media. Nowadays, though, many islanders, especially those who live on Inishmore and Inisheer, are bilingual.

For a time, in the 1950's and 1960's the future of Irish, as the first language of the islands, seemed to be in doubt. Many of the young people were leaving to go to English-speaking schools or to work in English-speaking areas, and Kilronan, the most anglicised village of the islands, was beginning to spread its influence to other areas.

In recent years, however, the islanders have become more hopeful that the language will survive. The Vocational School and the thriving fishing industry are attracting people from exclusively Irish speaking places to Kilronan and many of the Kilronan people are going back to the habit of speaking Irish. More and more young men and women are choosing to stay on the islands and Irish is no longer seen as being merely the language of the old. The establishment of Radio na Gaeltachta, the Irish language broadcasting service, has meant that the islanders' contact with the rest of the country through the media does not always have to be in the English language.

This change in the fortunes of the language is encouraging but the language can survive, in the long term, only if the community achieves a higher level of economic development.

REGIONAL DEVELOPMENT – THE FUTURE

The economic and social problems typical of the Aran Islands today are found, to some extent, on all the offshore islands and western seaboard areas of Ireland. Harsh environmental conditions, small farms and a lack of manufacturing industry have led to continuous emigration which the action of Government agencies has been unable to halt. The EEC has set up a Regional Fund to give a measure of special attention to such "problem regions" in Ireland and other parts of Europe and the Irish Government has offered special inducements to industries in order to attract them to such locations.

But the efforts which have had most success are those which came from within the local community. The people who live in underdeveloped regions are those best acquainted with the nature of their own difficulties and must play a major part in providing solutions. Co-operatives formed on the Aran Islands, for the development of the fishing industry and for the provision of essential services, have achieved significant results in the last ten years. They lack capital however and depend on the State to fund their projects.

The Irish Government is in the process of setting up Údarás na Gaeltachta (The Gaeltacht Authority), an organisation which will concentrate on developing Gaeltacht areas and co-ordinate local effort. The islanders believe that the tide of emigration is now, at long last, beginning to turn, and they look with hope to this new body to help them in their struggle for a secure and prosperous future for their community.

ACKNOWLEDGEMENTS

We would like to thank Ann Jackson and Brian Kavanagh for work in the development of the materials; Tim O'Neill for reading and commenting on the manuscript; for extracts from *The Islanders* by Tomas O'Crohan, by permission of the Oxford University Press; Dr. Brendan Kennelly for 'Sea'; for 'Years Later' from 'The Cleggan Disaster' reprinted by permission of Faber and Faber Ltd. from *Sailing to an Island* by Richard Murphy; for 'The Thatcher' reprinted by permission of Faber and Faber Ltd. from *Door into the Dark* by Seamus Heaney.

In instances where we have failed to trace the copyright holder, we would be grateful if they would contact the publisher.

We would like to thank the following for permission to reproduce photographs: Pat Langan and *The Irish Times*, pages 95, 98 bottom, 100, 113, 117, 119, 121, 133, 137, 149, 153, 159, 161, 168; Bord Failte Eireann 85, 87, 93, 98 top, 129 bottom, 157, 162; National Museum of Ireland 129 top; National Library of Ireland 106, 107, 111, 141, 145.

Other books from The O'Brien Press

AMERICA: A PLACE CALLED HOPE?
Conor O'Clery

The inside story of Clinton's America, written by an award-winning journalist. The book explores the issues which led Americans to elect the first Democratic President in twelve years, and looks at the reality of the American Dream today. From Palm Beach for the Kennedy-Smith rape trial, to the riot-torn streets of Los Angeles for the real story of the LA police, and behind the barricades in the war of the abortion clinics, Conor O'Clery reveals how the ordinary American has ben changed by these sensational events.
Paperback £9.95

THE HAUGHEY FILE
Stephen Collins

Love him or hate him, you can never be indifferent to Charles Haughey. Stephen Collins, political correspondent for the Sunday Press, reports on the former Taoiseach's extraordinary rise and fall - a career marked by intrigue, political machinations and a touch of the GUBU. The Boss's ability to survive became legendary, until an old scandal came back to haunt him...
Paperback £7.95

A VOICE FOR SOMALIA
Mary Robinson, President of Ireland

A first-hand account by the President of her historic visit to famine-stricken Somalia, including her day-by-day diary and her suggestions and hopes for the future.
Paperback £6.95

MARY ROBINSON

A President with a Purpose

Fergus Finlay

Fascinating account of the Robinson campaign. The making of a
President as it really happened.
Paperback £5.95

FOLLOW YOUR DREAM

Daniel O'Donnell

This is the story of a superstar. Daniel's story. It unlocks the door to his
private world, taking you back to his childhood years, through the
difficult early days on the road to his life at the top. Full colour
photographs.
Paperback £8.95

DUBLIN AS A WORK OF ART

Colm Lincoln

Dublin is the product of many hands and minds. Its streets chart Irish
history. This book follows that history of individual buildings and
streets. Over 80 black & white photos by Alan O'Connor complement
the text, some quirky, some serious, but all creating an intriguing
pictorial record of Ireland's historic capital city.
Hardback £19.95

THE STUNT

Shay Healy

Forget all that popstar do-goodery of U2 and Bob Geldof, *Poison Pig*
just want to get rich quick and have a good time doing it. And with their
slimy manager, 'Snake' O'Reilly, pulling the strings and organising the
ultimate publicity stunt, their dreams of the big time look set to become
real ...
Paperback £5.95

OLD DAYS OLD WAYS
Olive Sharkey

Entertaining and informative illustrated folk history, recounting the old way of life in the home and on the land. Full of charm.
Paperback £6.95

SLIGO
Land of Yeats' Desire
John Cowell

An evocative account of the history, literature, folklore and landscapes, with eight guided tours of the city and county, from one who spent his childhood days in the Yeats country in the early years of this century. Illustrated.
Paperback £9.95

WEST CORK WALKS
Written & illustrated by Kevin Corcoran

Experience the rugged wildness of Ireland's most southerly region in the company of an expert naturalist. Walking in West Cork offers an incredible variety of choice - mountainous peaks, rolling heaths, forested valleys, pristine lakes, sandy beaches. 10 walks, spread across West Cork. Caters for casual strollers, family groups, ramblers, serious walkers. Beautifully illustrated with maps and line drawings.
Paperback £5.95

KERRY WALKS
Written & illustrated by Kevin Corcoran

A superb walking guide to the wilderness and beauty of Kerry. Kevin Corcoran introduces Kerry's varied habitats and their wild inhabitants - heathland and bog, Ireland's highest mountains, coastal peninsulas, beaches, dunes, islands, forests, rivers, lakes. 20 walks. spread throughout the county. Maps, line drawings and colour photographs.
Paperback £7.95

WEST OF IRELAND WALKS
Written & illustrated by Kevin Corcoran

Explore the counties of Clare, Galway and Mayo in the company of a wildlife expert. The walker will experience the West's marvellous wealth of wildlife: hills and cliffs, bog, mountain, woodland, sea fjord, lake shore, beaches. Superb illustrations by the author, who is a biologist, naturalist and conservationist. The walks vary from gentle to tough, but most are moderate. There is a detailed guide on distance, time, and level of difficulty. Maps and line drawings.
Paperback £5.95

A Valley of Kings
THE BOYNE
Henry Boylan

An inspired guide to the myths, magic and literature of this beautiful valley with its mysterious 5000-year-old monuments at Newgrange. Illustrated.
Paperback £7.95

THE BLASKET ISLANDS
Next Parish America
Joan and Ray Stagles

The history, characters, social organisation, nature - all aspects of these most fascinating and historical of islands. Illustrated.
Paperback £7.95

CELTIC WAY OF LIFE

The social and political life of the Celts of early Ireland. A simple and popular history. Illustrated.
Paperback £4.95

TRADITIONAL IRISH RECIPES
George L. Thomson
Handwritten in beautiful calligraphy, a collection of favourite recipes from the Irish tradition.
Paperback £3.95

RHYMING IRISH COOKBOOK
Gordon Snell

Cookbooks you may have a-plenty,
Recipes both posh and plain
But here is one we guarantee
you will not see its like again!
Readers will follow them with ease,
These new poetic recipes,
And find, because they scan and rhyme,
They'll be remembered every time
This book will make a little treat
For those who cook - and those who eat
Paperback £3.99

LAND OF MY CRADLE DAYS
Recollections from a Country Childhood

Martin Morrissey

A touching and informative account of growing up in County Clare during the war years. Sensitive, detailed, moving story of a bygone era.
Paperback £5.95

THE CHANGING YEARS
Martin Morrissey

Sequel to the popular *Land of my Cradle Days*. The story of a boy hurrying towards adulthood in a rural community itself caught up in the march of progress towards a more modern Ireland. Martin Morrissey breathes life into the characters and customs of west Clare in the 1940s and 1950s.
Paperback £5.95

A PLACE OF DREAMS

The Lough Gur People

Michael Quinlan

Life in the New Stone Age was harsh and uncompromising. In this historical novel Michael Quinlan explores that life when a group o prehistoric settler sails from overseas and finds a beautiful but some times dangerous new land - Lough Gur, now an important archaeologi cal site. *Paperback £6.95*

SMOKEY HOLLOW

Bob Quinn

Worm's eye view of how children managed to survive parents in the dark ages before TV. Halfway between city and country, betweer domestic piety and street vulgarity, between Irish aspirations and Britisr acculturation, the Toner children, Bob Quinn's fictionalised version o his own clan, explore all these alternatives to the full.
Paperback £5.95

THE WIT OF OSCAR WILDE

Sean McCann

A new edition of this delightful and entertaining book on an unforgettable Irish genius.
Paperback £4.95

IRISH WIT

Sean McCann

Canny Irish wisdom and proverbs on those staples of pub conversation - religion, the law, literature, drink
Paperback £3.95

IRISH GRAVE HUMOUR

Raymond Lamont-Brown

Strange and wonderful epitaphs collected from Ireland's past.
Paperback £4.95

THE COOL MAC COOL

Legendary Celtic Hero

Gordon Snell

Illustrations by Wendy Shea

The life and times of legendary Celtic hero Finn MacCool, composed
in lighthearted verse.
Paperback £4.95

Please send for our full colour catalogue